"There is little more enjoyable for a writer than to read about the craft, especially when the book is fashioned with the grace and style of Robert Benson's prose. You don't even have to be a writer to savor this delicacy. Just do yourself a favor and settle in for a treat that goes down like dessert but is also full of nutrition. I read everything I can find on writing, and I loved this."

—JERRY B. JENKINS, novelist and biographer

"I love reading and spending time with what Robert Benson writes. I think it is because his words and God's Spirit meet and dance on each page. In this book Benson generously shares how writing becomes art. *Dancing on the Head of a Pen* is direction for struggling writers and balm for the bruised writer's heart."

—SHARON EWELL FOSTER, author of the Christy Award–winner *Passing by Samaria* and Shaara Prize–winner *The Resurrection of Nat Turner*

Dancing
on the
Head of a Pen

ALSO BY ROBERT BENSON

ROBERT BENSON

THE PRACTICE *of a* WRITING LIFE

Dancing on the Head of a Pen

WATERBROOK
PRESS

56281801

DANCING ON THE HEAD OF A PEN
PUBLISHED BY WATERBROOK PRESS
12265 Oracle Boulevard, Suite 200
Colorado Springs, Colorado 80921

Details in some anecdotes and stories have been changed to protect the identities of the persons involved.

Hardcover ISBN 978-1-4000-7435-8
eBook ISBN 978-0-307-45814-8

Cover design by Mark D. Ford

Published in the United States by WaterBrook Multnomah, an imprint of the Crown Publishing Group, a division of Random House LLC, New York, a Penguin Random House Company.

WATERBROOK and its deer colophon are registered trademarks of Random House LLC.

Library of Congress Cataloging-in-Publication Data
Benson, R. (Robert), 1952-
    Dancing on the head of a pen : the practice of a writing life / Robert Benson.
       pages cm
    ISBN 978-1-4000-7435-8 (hardback) — ISBN 978-0-307-45814-8 (electronic)
1. Authorship. 2. Creation (Literary, artistic, etc.) I. Title.
    PN149.B37 2014
    808.02—dc23

                                                        2014002683

Printed in the United States of America
2014—First Edition

10 9 8 7 6 5 4 3 2 1

SPECIAL SALES
Most WaterBrook Multnomah books are available at special quantity discounts when purchased in bulk by corporations, organizations, and special-interest groups. Custom imprinting or excerpting can also be done to fit special needs. For information, please e-mail SpecialMarkets@WaterBrookMultnomah.com or call 1-800-603-7051.

This book is for
Ms. Jones of Merigold,
who first suggested I write these things down.

It is for
Messrs. Grady, Fotinos, Major, and Cobb,
Mmes. Mao, Copan, Lind, and Clements,
who kept giving me chances.

And it is for all those
who hear the call to wrestle with words and
have the courage to tell the stories
that are the salvation of us all.

And as always,
it is for the Friends of Silence and of the Poor,
whoever and wherever you may be.

To condense from one's memories and fantasies and small discoveries dark marks on paper which become handsomely reproducible many times over still seems to me, after nearly thirty years concerned with the making of books, a magical act.... To distribute oneself thus, as a kind of confetti shower falling upon the heads and shoulders of mankind out of bookstores and the pages of magazines, is surely a great privilege and a defiance of the usual earthbound laws whereby human beings make themselves known to one another.

—JOHN UPDIKE, *Odd Jobs*

Contents

I

Dark Marks on a Page

On a Book About Making a Book

Putting a book together is interesting
and exhilarating.… It is life at its most free,
if you are fortunate enough to be able to try
it, because you select your materials, invent
your task, and pace yourself.

—ANNIE DILLARD, *The Writing Life*

"I THINK I HAVE A STORY TO TELL. I JUST DO NOT KNOW how to begin. Can you tell me how to write a book?"

Most often I hear such a comment during the question-and-answer session after I have given a reading or a talk. The question also appears in some of the letters from people who are kind enough to read my books and kind enough to write me after they have read them.

The question comes up more and more these days. The digital age has changed so many things about the way writers and publishers find each other and ferret out access to sales and media outlets. And more and more the writer must not only make the art but deliver the audience as well. The whole process can seem a little daunting.

I always take the question seriously. I was once in the same spot and grateful for any help that might move me along toward learning to get a story down on paper.

Henri Nouwen was right when he said, "As long as we have stories to tell to each other there is hope."

Sharing the things I know about how a person goes about telling his story seems only right. Perhaps it is even, as the old prayer book says, a good and joyful thing.

———

My father came into my office one day at the publishing business the family owned and handed me a stack of cassette tapes and a stack of manuscript pages, and then he gave me an assignment. "I met this young woman in Canada," he said. "I liked the things she was saying when she was speaking onstage, and I told her we would help her make a book out of it. I have been working on it some, but I cannot seem to capture it somehow. Why don't you give it a shot?"

The book I helped the young woman make in those

early days of my wordsmithing career is considerably different from the books now published under my own name. But it was the first chance given to me to learn how to make the only art I ever wanted to make—a book.

It was my first ghostwriting assignment. I was nineteen years old.

Many years and many books later, I found myself leaning on my best friend's doorjamb on a warm afternoon. I was half conversing about writing a book and half watching the roses blooming in our back garden. Out of one eye I was also watching the fountain beside the path that leads to the studio where I write.

I always enjoy conversations about writing and writers. To be sure, the first joy of keeping such a conversation going is rooted in the fact that any conversation that keeps a particular writer from the burden of trudging back to the studio and back to writing sentences is a welcome conversation. The subject hardly matters. What counts is the ability to put enough words into the air to delay the inevitable.

My friend told me about her recent conversation with a

sweet woman we both know. Our mutual friend had been thinking she might try to write a book. The two of them thought a book might be down in there somewhere, hidden in one of the stories of her life, but the one who aspired to be the teller of the tale did not know how to begin.

"What should I tell her?" my friend asked. "What does she do to begin? How does one go about writing a book?"

———

The summer sun dropped down another little bit, and to get it out of my eyes, I shifted from the left doorjamb to the right and went into my best artist-as-teacher pose.

"This is the first thing I would tell someone who wants to make a book."

And then I began to expound, and the first thing and the other nine or so went on for a bit. I am a writer. Embellishing is one of my gifts. I also know how to stall when my own writing is not going well.

I described the steps I take when I begin to make a book.

Some of them are habits stolen from other writers, writers far better than I am. Some of them are practices discovered on my own after years of dancing on the head of a pen. Some are disciplines I stumbled upon to feed both the caliber of the writing and the work of being a writer.

After some forty years and nearly twenty books, I have learned I do not know a lot about a lot of things, but I do know how to write a book.

———

At the end of the conversation with my friend, the speaker in me went for the cheap joke as always.

"Here endeth the lesson."

After the appropriate groan with the complimentary grin, she said, "Write all that down, and I will pass it along. I think it can help anyone who has a story and does not know how to begin. I think it might even help people who have been writing for a long time."

She has been in publishing for almost as long as I have

been writing. If she says an idea or two of mine might help someone, I say, with a proper nod to the legendary songwriter Paul Simon, "Who am I to blow against the wind?"

Hence, this book.

———

Sometimes the people who ask the question go on to say they are not sure they can be creative on paper every day. I tell them with all seriousness I am not sure I can be creative on paper each day either. Most of the time, writing a book more closely resembles digging a ditch than participating in some transcendent creative experience.

A pen and a keyboard and paper and ink are nothing more or less than the tools of a writer. They are to be regarded the way a construction worker regards a well-worn set of boots and a well-loved shovel. The tools simply remind the worker to get up each day and go back to work no matter how much or little progress was made the day before. I became better at the craft of writing sentences on the day I finally understood I was engaged in a construction project as much as an artistic pursuit.

Writing a book is nowhere near as easy as it looks and heaven knows not as easy as some claim. Writing a book is seldom easy, even for those who have written some of them.

———

Fellow writers still ask the "how do you write" question too.

Most of us who write are curious about, if not downright fascinated by, how other writers go about their work, especially those writers whose work we admire. We each have our own way of going about the work, a way we have figured out through trial and error over the years. But listening to someone else describe the tricks she uses to keep herself digging every day reminds us of what works for us, and what does not, and helps us remember to be attentive to the things we already know to do.

My friend who writes historical novels set in Scotland told me she plays Scottish music on the stereo while she writes. Her trick reminded me I need silence in order to write. The next afternoon I removed the radio from my studio.

Another writer told me he works best late at night, reminding me which time of day works best for me to put new words on blank pages. I went home and rearranged my calendar to protect those hours each day, the hours best suited to my taking up a pen and working along a few more words' worth in the ditch.

I know writers who work in hotel rooms and coffeehouses, in the hours between public appearances, and in the poorly lit seats on red-eye flights. They call it writing in the cracks.

I know writers who write first drafts by hand, writers who dictate first drafts, writers who type the first draft on old manual typewriters even though the *e* and *s* keys have been stuck for years.

I know writers who write three books in a series every year. I know writers for whom a book a year is the norm. And I know writers who sometimes go five or six years between manuscripts.

I know a writer who used to make notes and scribble sentences and ideas on the back of business cards and napkins. At the end of the day, he would put them in a drawer in his bathroom, along with his spare change. A full drawer signified the time had come to move the bits of paper to a grocery bag and put them under the sink. When he had two bags full of stuff, the time had come to try to make a new book out of the mess.

There are lots of tricks to writing a book. The ones I know best are the ones I use in my studio.

———

Any of us—writer, designer, potter, painter, sculptor, architect, and on and on—wisely studies the habits practiced by the artists who inspire us in the first place. Those habits can guide us as we try to learn to do the work ourselves.

I have done this as I have gone along, so my answers to questions about how to write a book are bound by certain limitations. The most obvious: I only know how Robert

Benson writes a book. My way has been cobbled together over the years as I've borrowed a practice from one writer, incorporated a discipline from another, listened to others as they described the way they do their work.

The way I write a book promises to work for only one writer—Robert Benson. Whether or not this way will work for someone else remains to be seen. In the end each writer will have to find his own way. Anything I offer is merely a starting point at best.

But knowing how to begin the writing can often be the hardest part, whether one is talking about a day's work or a week's worth, a sentence or a paragraph, a story or a chapter, the first book or a sequel.

The only thing that may be harder than beginning is continuing to write. To write every day, week in and week out, guided by some vision you know you may not be writer enough to reproduce anyway, is very hard. Painters say that the art on the canvas is never the vision that was in their minds when they began. It is the same for writers more often than not. What writers hear in their heads is not always what they manage to put on the page.

While I am not certain exactly how you come to these pages, how you get up in the morning to dig in the ditch you are currently digging, I can tell you what I do when the time comes to pick up my tools, pull on my boots, and go to work.

And maybe it can help.

———

My hope for this little book is that it will help you write one of your own.

If you are not sure whether or not you can write a book, this one will not answer the question. You will have to write a book before you will know. I do hope these pages will give you a way to begin to make dark marks on pages of your own.

If you already write and have habits and practices and

disciplines that have worked for you before, your practices may be very different from mine. These practices that keep me working may do little more than remind you of how your way of working suits you.

But if they remind you to practice more faithfully, more rigorously, more diligently, I will count the dark marks on these pages worthwhile.

———

May they be at least a place to begin. Or begin again.

"O begin," writes the famous preacher and author John Wesley about starting out on another mysterious journey of faith, a journey not dissimilar to writing a book. "O begin."

And now we shall.

2

Follow Your Nose

On Deciding What to Write

The absence of other voices compelled me
to listen more intently to the inner one.

—DORIS GRUMBACH, *Fifty Days of Solitude*

IN A HOT SUMMER SOME THIRTY YEARS AGO, ONE OF my brothers got married in Colorado Springs. We live in Tennessee, so a wedding in Colorado called for a serious road trip.

When the time came for the long drive to carry us all to the big day, a small caravan, led by my father, rolled out of the suburbs of Nashville and headed north and west to Saint Louis and then west across Kansas toward the Rockies. The drive was long, and the summer was hot, and the sun was brutal. My memory is that we could see the Rockies when we cleared the western outskirts of Kansas City, but it seemed as though the mountains kept backing up in the distance. I would not have been too surprised to have passed a wagon train along the way.

In those days I drove an MGB convertible. The length of the trip and the unreliability of the automobile notwithstanding, I insisted on driving the MGB to Colorado. I also insisted on driving with the top down the whole way. After arriving in Colorado Springs, I spent two days in bed suffering from sunstroke. Those who had suggested I might have been better served by the rental of a car with air conditioning were right, of course.

But I wanted the MGB there with me for a reason. When the wedding was over, I was ready to be alone and to wander.

———

On the day after the wedding, everyone else packed up and headed home to Tennessee. I put the top down and headed north and west with only the barest notion of where I was going.

I knew I wanted to go far enough north to cross the Rockies at Independence Pass. I knew I wanted to wander some blue highways until I had wandered my way into Wyoming.

Somewhere in the wild and woolly West, I planned to circle back in the direction of the sunrise and pick up some four-lane to take me back south to Denver and to the highways that would lead back across Colorado and into Kansas and Missouri and over the big river into Kentucky and home to Tennessee. Having just this vague plan, I took my leave from my family and started out with only a map and a convertible and a clear western sky. And this time with a hat and plenty of water.

I waved good-bye to the ones who sat comfortably in their machines with the factory air, and then I peeled out of the parking lot. My younger brothers were watching, and an older brother in a convertible needed to give the young folks in the RV something to cheer about. I rolled down the road, thinking no more than two or three hours ahead at a time.

In the next days I passed through some of the most astonishing country I have ever seen. And all I was doing was following my nose.

"This road will get me to the next little town, and I can have a bite of lunch and figure out where to head next," I muttered to myself.

Another day I cleverly deduced, "Dark will be here before I get to Medicine Bow, so I had better spend the night in the next town."

Watching rain clouds come screaming across the big sky one afternoon, I realized, "Gonna be messy to go all the way to Horse Creek, so I might as well stop in the next town and see if I can find a decent sandwich and a place to stay."

I spent a morning sipping coffee and sitting, legs crossed, on the sidewalk, watching people go by on the square in Aspen. My eyes were peeled for both John Denver and Neil Young, but I came up empty.

One afternoon I drove a two-lane road side by side with a railroad track through a canyon that had me dreaming of riding toward the Ponderosa with Hoss and Little Joe. When the track disappeared into a tunnel, the road ran out, and I had to turn around and go back. I ran out of daylight, but the joy of driving that empty road turned out to be well worth the time and the gasoline.

The next day I got so lost in the mountains I ended up lunching on Popsicles and crackers on the front porch of a one-pump gas station because the nearest restaurant was a hundred miles away.

In the end I always got where I was going for the night. A few days later I even found my way home to Tennessee.

———

A lot of years passed before I really began to write, before I ever hoped the Muse might visit me at all. But remembering my trip out West reminds me of something important in my life as a writer. I have noticed over the years that when the Muse finally shows up, I am usually wandering around.

Wandering through the books I read over and over, I stumble upon an interesting notion, and the next few days and weeks are spent thinking of what draws me to that notion, and then words begin to come.

Wandering through my old journals—I try to read one or two of them each year while on retreat—I am reminded of a forgotten bit of my life, and the once-lost story finds a home.

Wandering the sidewalks in our neighborhood or through the park a few blocks away opens up a way of seeing something I never noticed before, and a bit of light appears in the dark of what I am trying to write.

"To remain silent and alone is to be open to influences that are crowded out of an occupied life," writes Peter France in his book aptly named *Hermits*. Wandering around alone, in the absence of other voices, helps me find what I have to say, or at least what I have to say today. Tomorrow will be another day.

I rarely trust the Muse to show up on her own. I worry she has better things to do, better writers to inspire.

I do have complete faith that the best way to be found by her is to wander around, both literally and figuratively. If necessary, put the top down. Take a stroll through the park. Open up a book of quotes. Thumb through your journals.

If she is going to show up for me, it will be somewhere on the road between Horse Creek and Medicine Bow, between my house and the park, in the midst of the dance I do with the fountain pen on the page.

It will be when I am wandering, when I am following my nose.

———

When it is time to begin a book, when the blank pages are waiting and the fountain pens have been filled, I recommend you make the barest of plans you can, just enough to aim at what you are setting out to do. Too little direction and you might miss Medicine Bow. Too much planning and you can talk yourself out of turning onto the little unmarked road that leads to the left, along which may be the moment the whole journey will end up being about.

It helps to make a list of the stories you want to tell and

events you want to describe or the things you want to say. I find it is better to make a list rather than an outline. A list makes me feel as though I am writing a book rather than taking a correspondence course.

I think it wise to leave enough room to ramble around between stops to see what is there to be discovered. Or perhaps to sit in a square and watch people go by. It will not hurt to drive down a long road and have to turn around.

I like to have enough of a plan to know when one might be well advised to turn west into the sunset or stop for the night. But I also need to give myself the freedom to add a chapter or throw one away, to add a story or save it for another day.

A writer can dutifully follow a well-reasoned outline and end up missing the point. A writer can complete the assignment she set for herself and still not write the work she meant to write.

———

"The most demanding part of living a lifetime as an artist," writes the sculptor Anne Truitt, "is the strict discipline of forcing oneself to work steadfastly along the nerve of one's own most intimate sensitivity."

Solitude is likely necessary to be in touch with the things deep inside you. Silence may be required for you to hear what those things are saying to you.

Do not be afraid to be quiet. Never be afraid to be alone.

Wandering around in wide-open spaces, especially spaces offered by a blank page, may be the key to making some art of those things found in the silence and the solitude.

It may well be that such places are where the Muse chooses to drop by for a visit.

Whenever you get the chance or the courage, put the top down and follow your nose.

3

Go to Your Room

On the Discipline of Being a Writer

In spite of everything I shall rise again:
I will take up my pencil, which I have
forsaken in my great discouragement, and
I will go on with my drawing.

—VINCENT VAN GOGH

I ONCE SPENT A WHOLE YEAR PRETENDING TO WRITE A book.

The sweet lady I married would get up in the mornings and go off to the publishing company where she worked. I would wave to her as she pulled out of the driveway, then go back in the house and stand in the hall outside the little room where I was supposed to be writing. If I stood there long enough, I could think of some chores to be done around the house before I started to write. I would convince myself one or two of these chores would take only a few minutes and then I would write. Before I knew it most days, it would be time for lunch and time to start planning for supper.

We had the most highly polished silver in town that year.

To find silver in better shape from week to week required a visit to the sacristy at the cathedral we attend. To this day folks in the altar guild ask if I would like to join their ranks.

We also had ironed linens for all occasions, six new flower beds, the best-manicured lawn in the neighborhood, and no dust on any surface in the house. We had fresh shelf paper every few weeks, and all our books could be found neatly arranged in alphabetical order by author, in three sections no less—reference, nonfiction, and fiction.

What we did not have at the end of that year was the book I was supposedly writing.

"How did the writing go today?" came the question each evening.

"Oh, it's coming along," I would say.

"I cannot wait to see it," came the encouragement.

"Me either," I would say. But I would only say that under my breath, because I knew that so far there was nothing to see.

—

Any writer worth his ink stains can think of a small army of things to keep him from writing. If he does not have enough imagination to invent the excuses necessary to keep him from writing, he likely does not have enough imagination to write a book.

Any writer worth the paper he is working on will also discover that the truth that was the original spark of inspiration for the work is long gone, and he will begin to wish he had never even mentioned the idea to anyone.

Even once he begins the work itself, it will get muddled, and the literary lifting will get heavy. A moment comes when the writer clearly seems not to have enough talent or skill to fix what appears to be wrong with the blamed thing.

It could be that part of the secret to surviving the writing life is to keep so busy doing other things that one never has time to write.

Perhaps a new thesaurus or book of quotes will help, he thinks. That way he can ignore the work for a few days while waiting for the proper reference books to arrive. Meanwhile, the mulch does have to be raked again, the car has not been detailed in a week, and the gutters must have some leaves in them by now.

Dwell too long on what editors and publishers and book buyers will think of what you have written so far, and before you know it, a basket of ironing must be attended to and a stack of silver needs polish.

———

Every writer goes through stretches of time when it is hard to get up in the morning and go sit down and write. Some will not admit the difficulty, and others will outright lie, but when you can get a writer to tell some semblance of the truth, you will learn there are more of those days than days when a writer can hardly wait to get to the board and sit down and try to write.

"There is nothing more difficult than a line," wrote Picasso. And his did not even have to be readable.

Have enough days in a row when a writer cannot write, and she has wandered her way into what people speak of as writer's block. (Not a term you will hear this particular writer use. I do often find myself in a peculiar state I refer to as *writer's pause.* My experience suggests a pause of this sort can last a year or two. But I refuse to refer to it as a block.)

Not much is needed to strike terror in a writer's heart and keep her looking for anything to prevent her from going into her room to write. Sadly, the longer she leaves a work untouched, the more frightening the work becomes.

Pages with words on them are not so scary. She can always come along later and repair them. But the blank pages can paralyze her.

————

There are writers who are exceptions, of course, writers who seem never to be paused, shall we say.

I know one of them, the most prolific good writer I have ever known. She writes fiction and nonfiction. She writes for adults, for women, for young adults, for children. She writes quickly, and she writes well.

Some days I admire her discipline and her ability to produce good work at that pace and consider myself fortunate to be friends with such a prodigious talent. Other days I mutter her name under my breath, annoyed with her for showing up the rest of us, and then I go on to criticize myself for the snail's pace at which I work. She can turn out what I would consider to be a good day's work before I can finish a pot of tea.

On those days I hold on tightly to what Annie Dillard says of writers who pound out books in ridiculously short periods of time: "There is no call to take human extremes as norms."

———

At the beginning of a new book, I find it easier to write if I do not think about the fact I am attempting to write a book.

Who in the world needs another book anyway? There are thousands of good ones already, and some of the best ones have not been read by very many people at all.

A day spent reading Annie Dillard or Graham Greene or John Le Carré or Thomas Merton or Doris Grumbach or Frederick Buechner can convince anyone who wants to write that the good stuff has already been written and, in fact, so marvelously written that anything else by anyone else, including me, borders on being audacious at best and pretentious the rest of the time. Last week while reading Buechner, I realized that if I wanted to make a contribution to the literary world, I should do his laundry and mow his grass so he would have more time to write.

———

To say you are going to write a book sounds as though you are about to do something of weight, something worth doing in the first place, something deserving of being unleashed on the unsuspecting world.

It sounds as though you should know how it is going to turn out in the end, as if a clear thread runs from the moment of inspiration to the moment you write the first sentence, a thread followed logically and artfully and trium- phantly to the end. Such thoughts can make writers so ner- vous they tremble at the notion of sitting down to actually write.

Scarier and scarier the more I think about it. So I try not to think about it.

In fact, the more I think about writing a book, the more likely I will end up with not much at all on the page.

———

Toward the end of the Year of Pretending to Write a Book, an interview on *All Things Considered* caught my attention. The man being interviewed was described as a consultant and counselor to creative people struggling with the Afflic- tion That Must Not Be Named. He knew about this malady because he is a writer himself.

He talked about his work with musicians and screen- writers and novelists and painters. I was uncertain if he might have great wisdom to share with a butler and general yardman who was pretending to write a book, but I listened anyway. Listening to people talk about writing was as close as I came to participating in the literary life in those days. Listening to someone talk about writing was the only thing that made me feel like a writer.

I sat down to listen on the cool hardwood floor outside the room where I was supposed to be writing.

———

I paraphrase here, but his voice rings in my head twenty years later, even though I did not catch his name that day.

"Remember, you do not have to write a book today. There is not enough time to write a book today. You do have to go to work today.

"Go into the room, and close the door.

"Then before you do anything else or think about anything else, turn on the machine you use to do the work.

"Boot up the computer and scroll through until you are at the place where you stopped.

"Or take the cap off the pen and go to the spot on the page where you left off yesterday.

"Or put your hands on the piano keys and feel the cool of them under your fingers.

"Then repeat some of what you did the day before.

"Pick up the brush and spread a bit of the last color you used yesterday along a spare bit of paper or canvas.

"If you are a writer, type in the last few bits you wrote yesterday.

"If you are a composer, keep playing those last few bars over and over again.

"If you are an artist of any sort (writer, painter, composer, or such) and made for this work and meant to be doing it, then in two or three or five minutes, the working itself—not what you are making, but the physicality of making it (the mechanics, the process, the feel of it under your fingers)—will seize hold of you, and new work will begin to appear. Good, bad, or indifferent, in need of more revision or less, the work will take over. You will be working, you will be writing, and perhaps you will be writing a book.

"You do not have to write a book today," he said. "You have to go into the room, close the door, start your engines, and move your fingers until the working takes over."

I turned off the radio and went into my room and took the cap off my pen. By my lights, his wisdom has helped me make what is now approaching some twenty books in some twenty years.

I did finally learn that his name is Eric Maisel. The debt I owe him can never be repaid.

———

Ezra Pound once told a friend, "I did not enter into silence; silence captured me."

Eventually something just as magical may happen to writers if they go to their rooms and take up their tools each day.

Perhaps writing will capture them.

———

After all the years of enduring the Affliction That Must Not Be Named, I have learned to take one step in the right direction. I go into the room and close the door. I pick up the pen and begin to scratch across the paper. The sound of the nib scratching out words on the surface of the paper always captures me.

Before long, be the day's work good or bad, the work itself will draw me into it. I will look up, and I will be writing.

"It's just like bull riding," said the rodeo champion Ty Murray about an art he was trying to master. "You're never quite ready. It just becomes your turn."

4

Six Hundred Words

On Writing Every Day

———

The order of life, of occupation and work,
which you forced yourself to adopt when
you were seeking for grace, is also the most
helpful in prolonging within you the action
of grace which has now begun.

—ANONYMOUS, *The Art of Prayer*

THREE OF OUR BEST FRIENDS IN THE NEIGHBORHOOD sold their house and moved away. Not a good day, as I recall.

The three of them—father and mother and daughter—decamped to a little cottage in the woods about an hour from us, a cottage on his parents' farm.

The good news was that the move was temporary. They took the money from the sale of the house and bought a lot down the street from us and began building a new house. The foundation was laid around Thanksgiving, and our friends were to be out of the woods and back in the neighborhood in time for summer.

Most mornings in those days, when I would get in our

car to drive the few blocks to the store to buy the newspapers we read at our house, I would roll down the block to check the progress on their new house. It was out of my way a bit, but I was anxious for them to come back home to Sunnyside, where they belong.

Some days it seemed as though the construction crews had made no progress at all. Some days I despaired of there ever being a homecoming.

Waiting for my friends to return taught me something about the writing life.

———

Though the fact was unbeknownst to him, the late and great British writer Graham Greene is one of my teachers.

Mr. Greene's sentences and stories captured me as a reader. His eye and his ear caught my attention as a writer. I take up his novels over and over in the hope that the more I read them the more chance there will be I will finally learn to craft a decent sentence.

"Only after the writer lets literature shape her can she perhaps shape literature," writes Ms. Dillard.

———

Mr. Greene spent much of his life as a newspaper and magazine man. He also spent some years as an agent in the Foreign Office for the British government. Besides whatever clandestine work he was up to on any given day, his working days were filled with rewrites and deadlines and meetings and correspondence and travel. Somewhere he found the time to write hundreds of essays and reviews, twenty novels, three collections of short stories, three collections of essays, five plays, two autobiographies, one biography, and three travel books. All of which averages to about a book every year and a half or so for sixty years.

I believe he operated with the same twenty-four hours per day given to me. And to anyone else who would write.

One of his biographers tells of traveling on a cruise in the Mediterranean with Mr. Greene. After a proper British breakfast, the kind of breakfast you find on a ship whose name begins with the letters *HMS,* they sat down in lounge chairs on the deck to enjoy the sun and the breeze. The conversation slowed, a silence ensued, and Mr. Greene pulled out a little notebook and a fountain pen and scribbled for a while. After a bit he closed his book.

According to this account and according to his custom, he wrote exactly six hundred words and put the book away. Mr. Greene published about three dozen books.

Evidently, he wrote them six hundred words at a time.

———

Six hundred words a day does not sound like much.

(Right this moment we are only about six hundred words into this chapter, and you still do not know how my neighbors' house is coming along. Take a deep breath. Everyone will soon be back where they belong.)

If I said to you I was going to write only six hundred words today, you might consider me among the laziest of

writers. In my defense I offer this: six hundred words a day,
six days a week, for fifteen weeks yields a manuscript of fifty-
 ds, a book of 170 to 190 pages, depend-
e has been designed.

es is nothing so grand as a finished
pile has to be torn apart and put back
nd revised, generally half of it thrown
gs required to make a good book still
Such is the rest of the day's work for a

this: six hundred words a day for about four
leave you several months to do the rewrite and
ok within a year if you work diligently.
Good enough for Mr. Greene. Good enough for me.

———

A writer does not have to write a book tomorrow morning
when he goes wherever he goes when the bell rings to an-
nounce the time has come to write. A writer cannot write a

book tomorrow. A carpenter cannot build a house tomorrow morning either.

What a writer has to do today is write a few hundred words. And then do the same the next day and the next.

In his novel *All We Know of Heaven,* Rémy Rogeau writes, "Antoine likened monks to oarsmen on a ship, lifting a sheet to catch a sacred wind, the breath of something holy."

What a writer has to do tomorrow amounts to snatching a few hundred words from the wind.

———

My first draft of a book is written in longhand in little sketchbooks that are easy to carry so I can write my daily word count even when I have to be away from home. As long as I have a sketchbook and my favorite pen with me, I have all the tools I need.

Each day the job is simple. Go to a place where I can do the day's work. Take the cap off the pen. Open the sketchbook to where I left off. Write the next six hundred words. Close the book. Cap the pen. Pat myself on the head and go get newspapers.

The following day if I have trouble knowing what comes next, I will go back and read a page or two to myself.

If the work is rolling along smoothly when I get to six hundred words, I stop anyway, even if I am in the middle of a sentence. I know I have to come back tomorrow, and I discovered years ago it is better to come back to a place where I have some idea of what I am doing next. At the very least I try to leave myself midparagraph, the easier to know how to begin when I come back in the morning. I always try to straddle a gap between chapters so I do not get stuck not knowing how to start the next chapter.

Except for moments when I read a page or two from yesterday or the day before in order to jump-start myself, I never look back at this stage.

There are days when I write my six hundred words and am well aware that what I write is not as good as what I wrote a few days or weeks before. I notice the voice has gotten out of tune or the tone is wrong somehow, and no small amount of it will have to be fixed when it is time to rewrite.

"The feeling that the work is magnificent, and the feeling that it is abominable, are both mosquitoes to be repelled, ignored, or killed, but not indulged," advises Ms. Dillard. These early days, the beginning days in the work, are not the time for judgment. These are the days for trudging along, in my case six hundred words at a time.

At the stage where I am getting the first words down on paper, I take no chances I will talk myself out of writing all the way to the end.

———

The first lines of this book were written eight years ago on an island as I watched the sun burst out of the Atlantic. I watched it that morning and pulled out my pen and began. Same spot each day for almost three weeks, and then the same time each day for weeks after I was home in my studio and the morning view was not nearly so spectacular.

Six hundred words a day for a few weeks and months, a couple of years of the thing sitting in a drawer, a couple of years rewriting, and eight years later we have a book.

We know we have a book because something lovely is taking place just now—you seem to be reading a book I made, at least a few thousand words of it.

———

In the early days of a book, I am simply making a start to making a book. I put six hundred words a day on the blank pages before me.

The pile of pages I will have a few months from now, the ones with words on them, the ones I will have to work with when finished with this draft, are not scary. All they will need is attention and care and craftsmanship. No easy task, but not a scary one either.

The blank pages are always the most terrifying ones.

———

"To be an adult," writes Ms. Grumbach, "is to learn how to parcel out at the appropriate time a part of oneself."

To be a writer is to learn how to parcel out an appropriate amount of one's time each day that will yield the sentences that will form the paragraphs that will fill the pages that will lead to something that so closely resembles a book no one will know the difference.

Six hundred words a day works for me. More or less may work for you.

Writing every day is what matters, methinks. Daily, disciplined, thoughtful, tenacious, clear—write your words each day.

———

If you begin your book about the same time your friends begin construction on their new house down the block, you will have a book about the same time your friends come home.

And one fine morning when you roll down the street to

get the papers, they will be moving in. They will have furniture to arrange and things to unpack and a home to make.

And you will have a pile of pages from which you can craft a book.

Welcome home. To all of us.

5

The Jury Box

On Choosing an Audience

———

I have tried to write poetry for people
for whom there is no poetry.

—PHILIP LEVINE, in *The Hand of the Poet*

WHILE I WANDERED MY WAY THROUGH MY FAVORITE sections of my favorite bookstore one evening, a voice over the public-address system announced that the acclaimed southern novelist Doris Betts was about to read from and answer questions about her new book. I confess to knowing little about her or her work. But the woman to whom I am married and her book club friends—a dozen or so of the smartest women I have ever known, by the way—rave about her. So I wandered over to the place where famous writers read in the hope this not-nearly-as-famous writer might learn a new trick to make him better at the craft.

After Ms. Betts read from her book, she took questions

from the audience. Most of the questions were about characters and plot lines from previous books, questions asked by people who had been reading her novels for years. I kept listening because she was such a delight to listen to.

At some point I began to lose concentration. Probably I was surreptitiously glancing around the store to see if any of my books happened to be visible on the shelves, hoping that maybe even one or two might be face out, and so I did not hear the next question. But Ms. Betts's answer came to me as clear as a bell. And a door of some sort opened for me.

Ms. Betts said that when she writes, she writes for a jury of twelve. It was an entirely new notion for me. She went on to say that some of the same people are always in the jury. At least one of her parents is always there, because she wants to please them. Permanent seats are marked for an old friend or two as well. She fills the remainder of the seats in the jury with specific people she wants to hear this particular story—a neighbor, a friend, a teacher, another writer, a reader who wrote her a letter, a character from a previous novel who was modeled after someone she knows. Then she writes the book to them and for them. Maybe even *at* them on some days, if I may bear witness from my own experience.

———

Some writers I know say they write for themselves alone and if someone reads the work, they are appreciative. But they insist they are making the work for themselves. I understand what they mean. But I am another kind of writer. I do not aspire to being a tree that falls in the woods and no one hears.

I want to write. I may even need to write. But I want to be read as well. I want to be heard.

When I begin to write a book, I ask myself some questions. Who do I think might read the writing I am about to do? Who do I expect to be interested in the stories I am trying to tell? Who do I hope will discover and enjoy and be moved by them?

Once a writer discovers the story she wants to tell, she must figure out to whom she wants to tell it. It helps me to name their names.

———

On a retreat in Texas once, I heard Frederick Buechner say that he writes to people he loves and who really know him.

"You use your real voice with those you love," he said, "and you cannot be phony with those who know you well."

———

Since the chance encounter with Ms. Betts and the weekend with Mr. Buechner, I have never even considered writing to an audience. An audience is somehow faceless and forbidding to me. Whenever I try to write in the direction of an audience, the work comes out flat and forced. The only real way to write, at least for me, is to write to people I know and people I love.

———

So to begin a book, I select a jury.

I take a piece of paper, and as only someone who has too much time on his hands might do—a writer, for example—I draw a little box, divide the box into twelve squares, and write names in the squares.

No one knows better than I do how silly this sounds. (But then the whole notion of writing a book so that some person I have never met in some city I have never visited might pay twenty dollars for the right to take my scribblings home and spend hours reading them is not too far from silly itself.)

Certain names are always in my jury box.

My father has been gone for more than a quarter of a century now, but I do not want to write anything that would keep him from grinning at me with the grin that always made me grin back. The same is true for my best friend, the woman to whom I happen to be married.

My editor, a dear friend for years now, always has a seat in the jury box. When the work is done, I want her to send me one of her funny little notes to tell me how wonderful my work turned out. Even when the next thing I receive from her in the mail includes two dozen pages containing the hard truth about what has to be done in order to make the work good enough for other folks to read.

There is no need to try to fool myself. These are the people who love Robert the writer the best, and they are the people who are most likely to catch me if I do not write honestly. They are the people who know my voice better than anyone else. They are the ones most likely to notice when I am being lazy as I write.

Other seats in the jury go to people I want to *hear*—really hear—what I am trying to say in this new pile of words and sentences and stories. Some are friends of long standing. Some are people I met on retreats. Some of them have shared long conversations with me about the things we think matter at this moment in our lives. Some are people I have met only once or twice but with whom a sudden kinship formed.

Once I have written the names in the boxes, I paste a

copy in the front of the sketchbook I use for writing this particular book. I put another copy on the wall above my writing board. I look at the jury box every day when I go to work. I keep my eyes on the jury while I work, and they keep their eyes on me.

Then I begin to write.

I write what I think of as a series of letters, letters to people I know and people I love, people with whom I must use my real voice and people with whom I cannot be phony.

There are days when I am writing and wonder if a particular bit goes in or comes out. The jury always knows. I picture myself reading this bit or that one aloud to them, and I watch their faces to see whether or not I still have them with me. It helps me figure out a way to make the next sentence or two work a little better so they will not get lost in the text somewhere.

As Mario, the love-struck young man in *Il Postino*, aptly says, "Poetry doesn't belong to those who write it. It belongs to those who need it."

While what I write is not poetry, and it can hardly be regarded as needed, I believe in what he says. The writing is for the people in the jury box. It is not for me.

———

In a nineteenth-century book, Horatio Alger Jr. gave birth to the question "But will it play in Peoria?"

When I start to write a book, who knows if it will play in Peoria or anywhere else?

Writing is hard enough. Writing can be doubly hard when one tries to write to some unseen, unknown crowd of folks in Peoria or any other spot on the planet.

But I have come to believe that engaging the people who love you the most and the people with whom you cannot be phony makes it possible that an audience will see your work in Peoria or somewhere else.

Please the jury, and there is a chance your work will be seen by others.

Write for those you love; if you make them happy, they will tell someone how challenged or refreshed or empowered or reflective your words made them feel.

They will be gentle with you when you show them the work, of course, because they love you. They will also be the ones who let you know if your words are honest and true, and when they are not.

They may not be the most critical readers, but they will be the most important, because they will be the ones who keep you writing.

They are the ones who always grin when they see your words coming.

They will tell other people, and then those people will tell other people. Which is how writers are discovered and books are sold. Even to strangers in Peoria.

6

Speed Kills

On Place, Time, and Tools

———

The urge to get up and go is a temptation to
look elsewhere for what really is at hand.

—CAROL OCHS

I spent the first few years of my working life in marketing at the family publishing company, a learn-on-the-job, self-taught, make-it-up-as-you-go-along sort of person. When my time in publishing was done, I had to find another way to make a living.

Over the years I had written enough advertising copy to have what passed as a portfolio to show to potential employers. The only thing I knew for certain at the time was that I wanted to make a living putting words on paper.

A friend who owned a small agency in Chicago hired me as a copywriter, and I headed off to the "City of the Big Shoulders" to see if I could carry my weight in a city full of big-time advertising writers.

Two days into my time there came the first big revelation of my new career. Of all the things I had learned in my self-taught journey as marketing hero and budding copywriter, one thing I had never learned was how to type. Embarrassing to say the least, especially for an English literature major, part-time poet, and copywriter.

When I started to work at the agency in Chicago, I would get an assignment of generally around fifteen hundred to two thousand words, given the nature of the corporate communications work in which the agency specialized. I would gather the notes from the client interviews and the research calls and would write on a yellow legal pad with a Black Warrior number-two pencil. I would noodle on the assignment all day and, more often than not, end up taking the work home with me so I could scribble on it some more before I went to bed. In those days late at night was my favorite time to write. (Days were for going to see the Cubs at Wrigley Field or for walking through the Art Institute during baseball's off-season.)

My writing desk was an old pine table I had managed to

liberate from the publishing firm when I left Nashville. And I set it up in a corner of my living room.

My apartment was sixteen floors up in an old warehouse turned into apartments that looked south down Michigan Avenue and along the shore of the Great Lake itself, down toward Comiskey Park, the home of the Chicago White Sox. With binoculars and a clear night, you could see the lights of the ballpark and the top of the first-base dugout from the roof of my building. Nothing else in the park could be seen. But you could listen on the radio and watch the game in your mind.

I could also gaze out the west windows, looking over Congress Parkway, the one that runs under the post office— no kidding, under the post office—all the way west until the lights from the traffic faded. Cars disappeared into the darkness just this side of a flashing red light on the radio tower in Wheaton, more than twenty miles away.

Staring through those windows and down at those legal pads, I first noticed the ways in which the wheres and the hows of one's writing can affect the writing itself. With my elbows on the old table, my chin in my hands, my pencil in my fingers, the lights of the city below and beyond, I learned to slow down and take deep breaths and let the writing come to me.

I learned to allow as much time as it takes to make a sentence or a paragraph or a story come to life. I fell in love with the craft of writing. I had always loved the joy produced by writing anything someone else responded to, but in those days I learned to love the work itself.

And I learned the value of slow. I learned not to chase the words but to listen for them.

———

First thing in the morning I would write out a fair copy of the piece—*fair* being code for legible—and hand the pages to a young woman in our office who did know how to type.

After she typed the copy for me, I made changes with a red pencil. I passed the pages back to her, and she typed it again, and I scribbled on it some more, and so on. By the end of the second day, I had a clean draft to show my boss. The next day he fooled with it some. Then I noodled around on it some more. Then we sent a clean copy off to the client via messenger or overnight delivery, and everyone up and down the chain of command took out their pencils and tinkered with it some more.

By the fourth or fifth day, the copy went to the art director, then off to the typesetter, and back to me after a couple of days. I would mess with the words some more. (*Mess with* being the copywriter's term for rewriting.) Then the layouts would be finished. We would tweak it a little more, and finally everyone would sign off on it and declare this thing finished. We would cross our fingers and send it to the newspaper or the engraver or the printer.

After doing this work for a couple of years, I moved home to Nashville and worked freelance. It was just around the time that FedEx offered ZapMail. (For some reason FedEx owned all the facsimile machines in the universe for a couple of years.) You could be on the telephone with your client doing the research on Wednesday morning and learn that they expected to have the copy by the next morning even if they were hundreds of miles away.

Then everyone got a fax machine. So you wrote in the morning and were expected to deliver a piece to the client by the end of the day.

———

Freelancing finally ran its course for me, and I went to work for a small Nashville agency. After I signed the contract, I asked who would type my copy. My new employer just grinned and said we would figure it out.

When I got to work the next morning, a computer sat in the middle of my desk with a note attached that suggested I might want to learn to type things for myself. The computer on my desk was a 528 Macintosh from Apple, one of those big green dinosaurs. They put it on my desk and laughed at me when I said I did not know how to use it. A new world had landed on me with both feet.

I soon learned to hunt and peck with the best of them. But now I was to type a piece on Monday morning, have it approved by my boss on Monday afternoon, and meet with the client by Tuesday morning.

With the right software you could write the piece, set the type, and produce page proofs even as you wrote the first draft. You could be at the printer by Tuesday afternoon.

Thanks be, I fled the advertising business before Mr. Gore and his friends invented the Internet. A friend I work with wants me to sign up for a Google service so he and I can simultaneously edit the same piece of copy for his blog in the corner of our computer screens without even having to talk to each other. I do not believe this is the sort of idea I will come to love.

The work of writing sentences has gotten faster simply because it can be done faster. The work gets faster, but it does not necessarily make the sentences better.

Fast is a good thing, I suppose, if you are making ads or driving racecars or fixing lunch for hungry children at the beach. But it may not always be a good thing if you are trying to write a book.

———

Good writing takes time.

"Words not only convey something, but *are* something," observes Mr. Buechner. They "have color, depth, texture of their own, and the power to evoke vastly more than they mean."

Good writing needs time for the texture of the words to develop, for the momentum to build, word upon word, sentence upon sentence, scene upon scene, story upon story. A little air between sessions at the writing desk allows for each day's work to be greeted with a fresh eye and a full tank. Allowing the words to live there on the page for a while without being rushed off to the next stage too soon can help the writer when he comes to the pages again.

Time is the actual currency of the speed-worshiping age

in which we live and write and have our being. And time is the currency with which we write our sentences and stories. *Hurry* is not a proper posture for a writer.

———

I have a friend in the neighborhood who runs and lifts weights and does yoga. He has a steady job as well and gets his oil changed every three thousand miles and flosses his teeth twice a day. He does not mean to, but he makes me feel inadequate most of the time.

The other day he saw me walking quickly through the neighborhood, head down, a Yankees cap on my head. He thought I might be on the verge of actual exercise.

He said he liked watching me walk. "You are a determined little guy, aren't you?"

Determined is the proper posture for a writer.

———

In the middle of the last century, W. Somerset Maugham wrote, "I think I must be the last professional writer to write everything he has written with his own hand." Had he not passed away in 1965, I would write him and tell him I still carry on the fight to single-handedly restore the practice of writing books with a fountain pen.

I write the first draft of a book by hand most often at the blistering pace of six hundred words a day, an output many writers consider to be paltry. I refer to this first draft as the hand draft, for obvious reasons.

I then type the hand draft into the computer. As I still hunt and peck at the keys by and large, it can take me a while to do it. I have finally gotten fast enough on the keyboard to have bursitis in my thumbs. Which does not say anything at all about the caliber of the work but will at least get me into the category of writers known as determined.

My determined, slow, I-think-I-can, I-think-I-can way of writing has me rewriting a little as I type. Then I print out a hard copy and delete the computer file. (Yes, Virginia, I delete the computer file.)

I paste the hard copy onto the left-hand pages of a big sketchbook. Then I start to read it aloud, editing and rewriting and sorting and cutting and pasting as I go. The first time through I use a green pen, the second time a blue one, and the third time a red one. By the time the third reading is done, there is no more room in the sketchbook. The time for typing it all back into the computer has arrived. Once more the typing is slow, but it forces me to vote on every word and every sentence.

I got to thinking the other day about how many words I had written and how many sentences I had made. I started adding things up and discovered something unexpected.

I have about nine hundred thousand of my own words in print now, across almost twenty books. I also have thrown away almost four times as many words. And there are the quarter-million words in the back of a drawer, words I have never shown to anyone, and the half million or so that I talked myself out of writing before I even began. The above totals do not include the handwritten journals on my shelves—180 pages each, 125 words to the page, so almost three million words' worth of daily scribbling and wandering and word play and prayer.

Of the nearly eight million words that have floated through my head onto a page, some of which have been deemed publishable, I am happy with about four dozen sentences. Four of those sentences I think are especially fine. I weep whenever I read them in public, mostly at the thought of having been lucky enough for those words to have chosen me and for my having been smart enough to say yes to them when they came my way.

I am absolutely convinced of this: the more I am willing to go slow, to treat each blank page as gift, to pay attention to each word and each phrase and each sentence, and to be patient as they come to me, the more likely I am to wander into being the writer I am meant to become.

—

I would not go so far as to say all writers should write in this slow and painstaking way.

For starters, there are a limited number of colored pens and sketchbooks on the planet, and I need a lot of both to do my work. Too many of us writing books this way, and I will run out of supplies before I run out of sentences and stories.

I also have writer friends who make a powerful case for quick and dirty first drafts, for just getting sentences down on paper in order to have something to work with. Linda Clare writes, "Get the thing down as quick as you can; otherwise, you may never finish." I understand that.

But all first drafts are something less than wonderful most all the time. No matter whether one uses a fountain pen or a typewriter or a laptop to get the first draft down, whether one goes as slow as I do or not, the book is going to need a lot of work before it is done.

Going as fast as you can does not necessarily mean you are also writing as well as you can. Every writer's internal clock and writing pace will be different, but I do believe that always hurrying is not always helpful.

"I believe that the computer…," writes Ms. Grumbach,

"is now a serious enemy of literature." I believe she has a point.

———

One of my writing heroes is James Taylor, though our arts are different. He can carry a tune, for one thing.

"Sometimes a song will be finished for a deadline in the studio the day the thing is cast in stone forever," he once said, talking about the art of crafting pop songs. "I know that songs and arrangements evolve and develop over time," he went on, "that somewhere around the twentieth time it's played for a live audience, a song finally completes itself."

His art and the art I make are different, no doubt. If I learned nothing else from this fellow traveler with whom I have journeyed down different roads all my life, I learned this: if it takes twenty passes for a lyric of a few dozen words to grow into itself, then taking one's time with twenty or thirty or forty thousand of them is probably not a waste of time.

———

In the interest of full disclosure, I did once write a book using only a laptop—start to finish in just over sixty days. I had put off starting the project for months, and the deadline came crashing upon me, and I had no choice.

Some folks consider the book to be one of my best, though when I am on the road and read passages from it, I know it could have been better had I written it a little more slowly. Whenever I read from those pages in public, I still rewrite as I go. I heard a writer once say that a person never really finishes a book. She just finally has to send it in to the publisher.

Another five drafts or so, another five days even, and the book I wrote so fast might have lived up to the promise of the notion of it. The book always makes the readers grin about what they found on the page and always makes the writer sad about what might have been.

Mr. Taylor gets to perform his songs until they grow into themselves.

A book comes out exactly once.

———

You need not go as slowly as I do. But I recommend you not go as fast as you can. Speed does not mean the work goes better. Most of the time it only means the work goes faster. And speed can kill.

The value of slow is a lesson a writer does well to learn.

7

Hat Tricks

On Recognizing the Task at Hand

———

It is tempting, if the only tool you have
is a hammer, to treat everything
as if it were a nail.

—ABRAHAM MASLOW, *The Psychology of Science*

On a shelf in the little room where I write, there are three hats.

The first one is a black beret. If you could see me walking through the neighborhood wearing my beret and carrying my sketchbook, with my beard and my sunglasses and my sandals, you would say to yourself, "Now, there goes an artist if ever there was one."

"And a right stylish artist at that," some might say. I hope someone might say that.

The second hat is a sun-faded, well-loved, and well-worn New York Yankees baseball cap, my gamer from the last year the Yankees won the World Series. *Gamer* is the proper name for the new hat you buy at the beginning of the season. You wear it each time you watch your team play in the new season, or each time you listen to the team's game on the radio, and always when there is a chance you are going to bump into a Red Sox fan and you want to make a point.

The third hat is a brown fedora. When worn at the correct rakish, Indiana Jones angle, it makes a writer feel like a million bucks. The fedora suggests that I, the man underneath, am a man to be reckoned with, a man of action and decisiveness and clarity. A man who can make the tough calls and will do so gladly.

One of the tricks to making a book is to know which hat you are wearing while you are working on the different tasks required to make your book come to life.

———

When I begin to write a book, writing my daily word count with my fountain pen in my hand, following one sentence to the next, struggling to find the tone and feel and thread of a book, trying to discover what might be discovered at the end of the line of words, I am Beret Man.

In those early days, the heady days, the days when I feel as though I am an actual artist, going to work wearing such a stylish chapeau is in order.

The first trick is to keep the artist working.

When I have my beret on, I do not look back at the work as I write. If I criticize and edit and point out the flaws too soon, I can dampen my spirit and discourage myself before I have a chance to discover what it turns out I am trying to make.

I already know better than anyone that much of what Beret Man writes at this stage will reveal itself to be not good enough to be read by anyone. But many of the holes the new book has can be fixed later. Right now nothing can be allowed to get in the way of this new thing.

I do not bother Beret Man with the hard work of craftsmanship required to turn a pile of scribbling into a book that someone might want to read. The time for rewriting will come soon enough but not until the man in the beret has finished.

"Writing anything," as Gordon Lightfoot once observed about the art he made brilliantly for so many years, "is a fragile magic at best." He and Mr. Updike may or may not have known each other, but they were clearly on the same page.

Criticize the man in the beret too often or too soon or too harshly in the beginning, and he will put down his pen, afraid and discouraged and hesitant. It is right to leave him alone a bit, let him believe the work is golden.

Soon enough the truth will be apparent.

———

The truth will arrive when the time arrives to move on to the next part of the work—the rewriting, the editing, the second draft, and the third one, and the fourth one. Seven or eight drafts is not uncommon for certain writers who live in Sunnyside.

When the rewrite time comes, you put your gamer on. You jam the gamer down on your head and set yourself to work. The *artiste* who wears the beret is to be banned from the premises. The work is no longer golden. You are about to try to coax a book from a pile of unruly sentences. Sentences that merely hold some promise is often the best one can say for them.

A chest protector and a set of shin guards turn out to be helpful. Wristbands are not untoward. Spikes are not out of the question. Some of the so-called golden work must be thrown out altogether, never to be seen again. Other parts must be strengthened and moved and recast and pounded on with great fury until they are right.

A chapter's worth of pages must be laid out on a table, and sections and paragraphs and lines are moved from one place to another. Chapters themselves get shifted around in search of the order that works the best.

I have a list of words, lovingly referred to as the search-and-destroy list, that I tend to use over and over—weak verbs, lame adjectives, vague nouns. I go through the entire pile of pages with a fine-tooth comb and a decent thesaurus, eliminating weak words and looking for stronger ones.

This is not work for the faint of heart. This work calls for people who do not mind if their gamer gets dirty and sweat stained and faded. What happens in this stretch often results in more words on the floor than on the page.

This is craft, not art. This work will make the book or will break it.

You do not whistle while you do this work. You mutter and scream and growl. You roll up your sleeves and go to work each day prepared to fight with and for each and every line and all that is in between.

I spend a lot more time in my baseball cap than in my beret. Which is one of the reasons I keep two books going almost all the time. I walk to a nearby coffee shop and order a café au lait while wearing the aforementioned beret. I do not like café au lait, but I like being a man who can order one and do so with the accent on the proper syllable. I get to wear my beret for at least six hundred words each day and remember I am an artist.

The rewrite work requires my Yankees cap and my butcher's apron. I live a part of my day for weeks on end in a literary MASH unit equipped only with colored pens and an X-Acto knife.

———

Fedora Man has to turn up for an hour or two every day as well. He is the one who follows what goes on in the publishing world outside the room where Beret Man and Gamer Man have been hard at work. He is the one who worries about whether the thing will ever be published or read. Fedora Man must be listened to but not too soon.

Let him into the room before the right time, and he will discourage Beret Man. "No one will ever read this, you know. It is nowhere near good enough," he will mutter, and the artist in the beret may lie down and never pick up the pen again.

Let him in too soon, and he will tell Gamer Man he cannot possibly finish on time or maybe at all. He will wake up Gamer Man in the middle of the night to tell him someone else has already said all there is to be said about the book's subject. Well-loved Yankees cap and shin guards notwithstanding, Gamer Man is kidding himself, he will say.

The man in the fedora is the man you need when the work is done, and not a moment before.

If you are just starting out in this life, Fedora Man is the one who learns to write a synopsis and masters the art of writing proposals and composing cover letters. When you are a little further along, he talks to agents, wrestles with titles and catalog copy, weighs in on cover art and marketing plans.

There is a time and a place for Fedora Man. The trick is to know when he should be invited into the room.

You may think I am being overly dramatic. I can name a dozen talented writers who let Fedora Man into the room too soon and never picked up a pen again. They are people whose stories never got told because they had on the wrong hat at the wrong time and talked themselves out of finishing.

A loss not only for them but for all of us who needed to hear the story they might have told.

I keep all three hats on a shelf in the room where I write.

They are in front of me to remind me of all three parts of the work a writer has to do. I want to know which part of the work is on my plate this hour, this day, this week.

The hats remind me to be gentle and free and generous and kind to the artist I am trying to be when I am wearing the beret.

They remind me to be diligent and hard working when I have on my gamer and am trying to make something readable of the supposedly golden stuff handed off to me by the man in the beret. Especially when the stuff turns out to be not so golden after all. Some portion of it may yet shine before all is said and done, though hard work will likely be required for a few weeks or months.

Maybe it can be pounded into shape some fine morning before the man in the fedora shows up. The fedora reminds me that every day I have to do some of the things I am not always excited to do in order to find the book a publishing home and an audience.

The hats remind me to do the work that needs to be done next.

A writer has three jobs. Write the work. Make the work as good as possible. Find the work a home and a crowd of folks to love it. It helps to remember which hat I am wearing as I go along.

8

Under the Influence

On Reading to Write

———

Everywhere I go I find a poet
has been there before me.

—SIGMUND FREUD

My paternal grandmother was one of the people who taught me to love words and sentences and stories.

Her name was Jimmie Lou Root, a proper name for a pretty girl from southern Alabama if I ever heard one. When my first book came out, I drove to her little house, fifteen miles or so north of mine, to give her a copy. I remember her joy at holding it in her hands and her grin in my direction.

By the time that proud day came, she could no longer see well enough to read, so I read most of the book aloud to her. Two weeks later I went into a friend's recording studio and made her a private-edition audio version. She thought my being a writer was such a fine thing, and she told me so every time I saw her. At which point Miss Jimmie Lou always got my grin in her direction.

When she passed away, one of my aunts called with news that my grandmother had left something for me, and I would need a vehicle larger than my little convertible to carry it home. A few hours and a borrowed pickup truck later, my hallway became the new home for a set of three waist-high pine bookshelves my grandfather built for the last little house the two of them lived in together. A fine gift, from him to her, and from her to me.

Poet, printer, storyteller, publisher—my grandfather loved words and stories and paper and ink as much as anyone. Along with Jimmie Lou, he raised five children, one of whom was my father, the first poet I ever really knew. My first favorite writer, in fact.

My father seemed to have a knack for stumbling onto books by new writers, new voices. As his own family grew, his study was converted into a bedroom for me. His book collection stayed put, and I would read the books he brought home by the light of a little lamp on the bookshelves beside my bed. I rarely turned off the lamp even when I was about to fall asleep.

I still keep a small lamp lit in the central hallway of the little house where I live. It sits on the top of the shelves my grandfather built, shelves that are crammed three deep with books. But the light of the lamp illuminates a single row of books held in place between two triangular marble bookends. The row contains a selection of my favorite books by my favorite writers, some of which are from my father's collection. The lamp stays lit all day and all night.

My grandparents and my father introduced me to some of the writers. Others I managed to find on my own, but I was clearly drawn to them by the way their work lay down comfortably beside the books I had been reading all my life.

The other evening I noticed the way the light of the lamp fell on them. And then I realized the way the light from those writers had fallen on me.

"I went back to the book I had been reading, Elizabeth Drew's *The Modern Novel*," writes Doris Grumbach, "in which she says that 'the test of literature is, I suppose, whether we ourselves live more intensely for the reading of it.'"

———

The writers of these top-shelf books are my teachers, the ones I turn to in order to learn how to write. They are the people whose work has shaped not only my writing but my thinking and my spirit. They have no idea they have done such a thing to me, save the one I met twenty years ago and with whom I exchange letters on occasion.

Some of those top-shelf books are on writing, though only a few of them. Others are autobiographies whose pages describe the joy and the cost of living the life of a writer. A handful are collections of essays or volumes of poetry. There are a few novels there too, one or two of them perfectly written, at least by my lights.

Any writer should have a shelf of such books. He need not read the writers I read. But he should never forget that we are all going to write under the influence of someone.

Better for him if those writers are better than most. At the very least they should be the ones who make him want to lie down and take deep breaths before taking up his pen. Those are the books that will make him live, and write, more intensely. Reading anything less will not help him grow as a writer.

A direct relationship exists between the caliber of the writing you read and the caliber of the writing you make.

———

For those who are keeping score at home, these are the people who take up the most space on the top shelf in my hallway.

A Belgian priest named Louis Evely published a book in the sixties called *That Man Is You,* a book given to me to read as part of a discipleship class when I was in high school. Whatever influence Father Evely had on my spiritual journey, his most powerful influence on me came from the blank-verse style he used to write the book. I do not write in that form anymore, but the blank verse taught me how to take sentences and paragraphs apart, how to break them into separate pieces and see how they fit together to make writing that can be heard when someone reads the page.

Some of Frederick Buechner's books are on the shelf. *Now and Then,* one of the deeply moving autobiographical books he has written, taught me a seminal truth. "Listen to your life. See it for the fathomless mystery that it is," he writes. "In the boredom and pain of it no less than in the excitement and gladness: touch, taste, smell your way to the holy and hidden heart of it." For better or for worse, I have spent a lifetime doing that, and doing so on paper in the hope that others might come to listen to their lives as well.

Three by Annie Dillard—*The Writing Life, An American Childhood,* and *Teaching a Stone to Talk*—taught me to write as directly as I can, though I do not always live up to the challenge. She taught me to connect one story to the next until a whole comes forth.

Letters to a Young Poet is there, a tiny volume containing half the correspondence between the early-twentieth-century Bohemian-Austrian poet Rainer Maria Rilke and a poet-to-be. The latter kept the letters from the great man, not the other way round, and those letters later found their way into publication. Whenever I want to turn in my pen and my poetic license, I read Rilke's letters, get a good night's sleep, and get up in the morning and go back to scribbling.

John Le Carré and Graham Greene are two legendary British novelists. Many people know the former because of the fictional spymaster George Smiley, a character portrayed by Sir Alec Guinness on PBS. Mr. Greene's work runs from crime to intrigue to war to satire. I started out reading both of these writers as "entertainments," Mr. Greene's term, and finally came to realize they were both teaching me to look for light in the midst of the darkness that seems all around us.

My journey in the direction of learning to pray eventually led me to Thomas Merton. I do not go anywhere without a copy of *Thoughts in Solitude*. Sometimes kindly picking me up when I am discouraged, sometimes gently reminding me that this work is not life and death, he always reminds me that I am only making sentences here. Not life and death by any stretch.

Darkness Visible, the slim book written by William Styron about his struggles with depression, helped save my life. I first read it when I was in a psychiatric ward. I recommend the book to writers because so many of us struggle with this particular disease whether or not we know it, admit it, or deal with it. Styron helped me do all three. And with great power he taught me that if you are going to write a memoir, it is only right to tell the whole truth and nothing but.

Shelby Foote's three-volume history of the Civil War began its life as an assignment to write a short popular history of the war. Over twenty years it became his life's work and thousands of pages long. He takes an old story with an ending we already know and retells it so compellingly that we are deeply engaged in the story again. Not a bad model for anyone who writes about religion from time to time as I do, writing based on a Story most of my readers know by heart.

Doris Grumbach's memoirs teach me to pay more attention to the daily in my life, attention to the seemingly inconsequential, attention to which things actually receive my time and my energy and my art.

The twenty-one novels Patrick O'Brian wrote about the Napoleonic War adventures of Captain Jack Aubrey and his ship's surgeon, Stephen Maturin, caught my eye and ear a few years ago. About the fourth time through them, I realized that even though the Aubrey novels had been categorized as adventure, they were really books about a friendship between two men. I read them every year now. If I cannot learn to be a better writer, I hope to learn to be a better friend.

———

"Poetry is the spontaneous overflow of powerful feelings," writes William Wordsworth in his preface to *Lyrical Ballads,* essentially the opening sentence in Romantic literature. He goes on to say that a poet does not see or hear or feel things that others do not see or hear or feel. What makes a person a poet is the ability to recall what she has felt and seen and heard. And to relive it and describe it in such a way that others can then see and feel and hear again what they may have missed.

———

I turn to these writers and their pages again and again. They are my teachers. Though not all of them are poets in the rhyme-and-meter sense of the word, they are certainly poets in the Wordsworth sense of the word. And heaven knows they are better writers than I will ever be.

Grateful is the only word I know for the glimpses they have given me of what it means to attempt the work and live the life of a writer.

I keep these books close at hand because they help me remember the very practical things I tend to forget.

They remind me to pay attention to the stories of my life so that in the telling of them I might help others recall the stories of their lives, which is where the real truth of their lives is revealed.

They push me to make sentences that people can hear as well as read, to work as hard as I can until the whole of what I am writing becomes as clear as I can make it. To not give up on the work even when the work seems clearly impossible to write.

They help me remember, in whatever story I am writing, to look for the light in the midst of the darkness. To pay attention to the larger world around me, not just the world I call my own.

They push me to tell the truth, the hard truth about my life, as someone may be dying to hear it. To tell the old stories when the time comes but make them come alive. To not be so busy being an artiste that I forget to be a person and a friend.

———

This little row of books holds the best stuff in the world for me. This writing, as a friend of mine once said about some writing she loved, "touches the best in me and makes all that is less than my best better for having read it."

Even though I have read them over and over, they make me want to get up in the morning and write my six hundred words.

They give me the courage to rewrite and rewrite until I have done the best I can do. They remind me my writing might matter somehow.

I try to make sure I read some of this good stuff every day. Or every night.

I keep them under the lamp in the hallway so I can find them when I am in the dark.

———

I have very specific ways I read to feed my writing.

I consider a day without working the crossword in the *New York Times* has been lived considerably less than to the fullest. I can live for a day without sunshine, or orange juice for that matter, but a day without a shot at bringing famed puzzle master Will Shortz to his knees is hardly worth living.

I find it better to read autobiography or memoir by day and fiction or history by night. The daytime reading helps me to focus, to concentrate, to do the writer's work before me on any given day.

On discouraging days Herr Rilke will remind me why I write. The Reverend Buechner will point out that a small episode in my life that I am journaling may well reveal something important if I keep scribbling.

Ms. Dillard will kick me in the pants. "Draw, Antonio, draw, Antonio," she says, quoting Michelangelo. "Draw and do not waste time." I can hear the rest of her admonition even though she has never spoken to me—"Write, Robert, write. Write and do not waste time."

The night reading helps me to rest and to wonder and to wander and, perhaps, to dream. I believe I sleep better after sailing the seas with Captain Jack and Dr. Maturin and Mr. O'Brian, after staring down Karla with Smiley and Le Carré, or after wondering with Mr. Foote at the courage of those who charged across a Pennsylvania field on a hot July day at the behest of General Pickett.

Reading these writers gives me time away from the places and things and people I am writing about. The rolling seas, the streets of Berlin, the battlefields of our own sweet land keep me from staying too hunkered down in the work I must tend to on my board tomorrow morning.

———

For many writers what we do *not* read when we are writing can be as important as what we *do* read.

What I absolutely do not read when starting something new is anything even remotely related to whatever I am working on. If there are things I need to research before I write about a particular subject matter, I try to do the research long before I begin to write.

Reading the latest best-selling book on prayer while trying to write a book about prayer is not easy for me. Writing poetry while reading Rilke will undoubtedly end with my making no poetry at all. If I ever take a chance on writing the two novels I have been carrying around in my head for years, I anticipate a five-year hiatus from Le Carré and Greene and O'Brian will be necessary.

Day in and day out, at least for this writer, approaching original proves difficult. It is hard enough to keep piling one sentence on another without the added burden of feeling as though I must measure up to a passage clearly superior to what I am trying to make.

I think I agree with the critic Clive Barnes: "The job's impossible, and one must pray that one will be only moderately incompetent."

Reading work that constantly reminds me I will never measure up discourages me when I am trying to make something new.

Reading great work in the field in which I am working can end up skewing the sound of my voice, twisting it ever so slightly into what sounds like a poor echo of the voice of someone whose work I admire. Reading such work at the wrong time can make it hard for me to make work of my own.

To be a writer and not be under the influence of other

writers is impossible. But I recommend you go carefully. Pay attention to who you read when you are writing. Pay attention to how the light in the hallway falls upon them and how it falls upon you.

———

After many years of reading these same writers, I realize they have been preaching to the choir all along. Or at least the portion of the choir that first robed up, so to speak, in the late of the nights in my father's study when I was young.

I have now traveled far enough to know that preaching to the choir remains the best way to get the choir to stand up and sing.

Or to sit down and write.

And maybe to learn to write well enough that the work will sing on the page.

9

Working in the Cages

On Habits to Keep a Writer Sharp

———

At its best, the sensation of writing is that of
any unmerited grace. It is handed to you,
but only if you look for it. You search, you
break your heart, your back, your brain,
and then—and only then—it is handed to
you.… It flies directly at you; you can read
your name on it. If it were a baseball, you
would hit it out of the park.

—ANNIE DILLARD, *The Writing Life*

At least twice a month I am asked a version of the same old question by one of the regular cast of characters who are in my life. First, we catch up on the news with each other.

"How are the kids?"

"Are you still headed south to the islands in the fall?"

"Are you playing any golf?"

"How 'bout them Yankees?"

A moment arrives when we ask each other how work is going. I ask them about the company they work for or about the new job or about the church they pastor or about the school where they teach. The only person I never ask the work question is a friend of mine who is a private investigator. I never ask him anything about his work, though I bet he has some really good stories.

Eventually my friends aim the work question in my direction.

"Are you still writing?" is what they always ask me.

A series of decidedly witty answers goes through my head quickly.

"Yes, I am not allowed to do anything else."

"Why not, it beats working for a living."

"The White House job has been taken."

"I have been told I am not qualified to be a bishop in the Anglican Church."

I generally restrain my inner smart aleck for the moment and mumble my usual response. "Yes, I am still writing. Unbelievable, huh?"

No one ever asks an architect if he is still designing buildings or a teacher if she is still going to school every day. No one ever asks a pastor if he still drops by the church from time to time or a doctor if she still sees patients.

Writing a book is so foreign to many folks it is evidently hard for them to grasp the notion that one might do it more than once.

Whether working on a book at the moment or not, a writer should always be writing.

———

I wrote a book about baseball once, a set of stories built around one game at our local minor league park.

It pleased the folks who owned the team, and they sold autographed copies of the book in the merchandise shop and even let me throw out the first pitch one night. I threw a strike, a proud moment for a man who feared he might blow his only first-pitch chance, and a blessed relief for my teenage children, who feared the eternal embarrassment of having an old guy for a father who could not throw the ball on a line for sixty feet.

For several years the management allowed me early entrance to the games, even allowed me to use the players' gate behind the stands along the left field line. The ushers and the staff would wave me through as if I was somebody.

"Are you still writing?"

As long as they treat me like this at the ballpark, I would sometimes think.

Three or four hours before a game, a series of practice cages was arranged along the concourse for batting practice.

In one cage a player had a length of strong rubber bands with one end connected to a fence post and the other end connected to one of his wrists. He faced away from the fence and swung his arms and hands slowly, over and over, through the strike zone. He was not even holding a bat. Then he put the band on the other wrist and repeated the motion. He swung smooth, not hard. He was not trying to hit the ball out of the park. He was trying to build muscle memory for when the time came to hold a bat and swing hard, maybe even swing for the fences.

In the next cage a player hit balls off a tee, the same way five-year-olds do in the Tee Ball leagues, where they are first taught the game. He would hit the ball, and a coach or a teammate would set another ball on the tee. Fifty swings, maybe more.

Soft toss took place in another cage. A hitting instructor sat on a stool, a bucket of balls within reach, and slowly tossed the balls one at a time into the strike zone for the player to hit. The instructor sat to one side so as not to get killed while the hitter pounded away, trying to groove his swing for certain parts of the strike zone. The closer he got to the groove, the softer the sound of the bat on the ball.

In the next cage a man swung a long stick with a cord attached. At the end of the cord was a baseball. As the coach swung the stick, the hitter swung the bat, trying to make solid contact with the ball. The sound of the bat on the ball became louder in this cage.

Finally, a hitter got his chance to go into the batting cage and take live pitching on a real diamond. By the time he arrived there and made his three- or four-dozen swings, he would already have practiced his swing three or four hundred times in the hour or so before.

A professional hitter does these things every day to get ready for the fifteen to twenty times he will swing a bat in the day's game. Those seemingly little bits of practice in the cages are what prepare him to do the real work.

"Are you still writing?"

I'd better be, I always say to myself.

———

I am always writing but not always writing a book. Days come when I am hitting in the cage, trying to stay sharp. I try to keep my swing grooved so when game time comes, the time to write a book, I am as ready as I can be.

I scribble away on other things, trying to keep my swing up to snuff.

I recommend all writers do the same.

———

I suggest journaling for one thing.

I began my first journal when I was twelve. I started out using an ugly little paperback with a Peter Max cover that my father gave me for Christmas. Over the years I have come to fill about two sketchbook pages a day with notes and comments, observations and wondering, thanksgiving and tirades.

The stillness and the quiet inherent in this daily exercise can help a writer stay in touch with what is going on in his heart and mind in the hours and days and weeks of his life. The simple act of reporting to himself helps him learn to talk straight about things that matter. A journal forces a writer to listen to his life.

A journal provides a place for him to learn to speak truth to himself about himself or discover his capacity for disingenuousness. A place to discover when he writes too fast or too glibly, too carefully or too safely. A place to discover his voice slowly over time so that when the real game is afoot, he can trust it.

"The more faithfully you listen to the voice within you,

the better you hear what is sounding outside," writes Dag Hammarskjöld. "And only he who listens can speak."

———

I also recommend other writers be a bit of a pack rat.

I collect three specific writerly things. And I fool with each collection a little bit almost every day.

When I began working in advertising, practicing the craft daily, I learned to keep what is referred to as a swipe file. Every time I came across a particularly well-written or clever print ad, I would tear the page out and throw it in the swipe file. From time to time when sentences were hard to begin to write, I would thumb through the file, reading the good stuff until motivated enough to at least pick up the old Black Warrior and have at it. Stealing someone's idea was never the plan. Stealing the energy to find my own idea was the object. And it often worked.

So I keep a swipe file still, two of them. One in a folder in my desk for the things I tear out of newspapers and magazines or photocopy from books, and one on my computer for the things I download from the digital universe. (There, I used the phrase *digital universe* in a sentence without feeling pretentious. And I spelled *pretentious* without having to use my digital dictionary. My two parallel worlds seem to be running along nicely just now, thank you very much.)

———

The second collection I keep is a book of quotes.

People who have those little calendars with a quote for the day are behind before Lent comes every year. There are too many good sentences in the world. So I keep a book of what I call the "quote for the quarter-hour."

I keep the quotes in a computer file and add to them as days go by. I print the collection every couple of months or so and put them into a notebook I can thumb through in the quiet of an early morning when looking for wisdom. I also read through those pages when I am writing and looking for words I cannot seem to find or when I am on the road and folks I am speaking to are hoping for me to say something wise.

———

I am a wee bit embarrassed to confess the third set of things I collect. I call it the spare-parts file.

When the man in the gamer comes along and begins to hack away at the book I am making, cutting away the obviously dying and dead wood, slashing away at overwritten parts, tearing away unnecessary stories, I end up with a pile of words on the floor. I know those words do not belong in the book I am writing at the time. Even the man in the beret has given up on them by now. But letting go of them altogether is more than I can do.

So I print them out and hit them with a three-hole punch and stick them in a notebook. I whisper condolences to them as I do. "Your day will come," I tell them. Sometimes it does.

———

These three collections of things are often where I start on days when I cannot seem to start.

A line in a story by a theater critic in the *New Yorker* yields the beginning of a chapter. An odd requirement for twelfth-century monks living under *The Rule of Saint Benedict* opens up a whole new way of thinking about what I hope to become and what I hope to write. An old story of my own, discarded at some point, doggedly rises from the cutting-room floor to become the starting point for a new chapter in a new book.

———

Collect stuff that moves you, I say.

Collect it in whatever makes sense for you—a notebook or a folder or a computer file. Keep these things close at hand, and spend a few minutes with these favorite things every day. Ponder these things in your heart is a good bit of advice I got once from an ancient book.

These things may have some power to shape you as a writer. And some of these things you treasure may well come back to help you move your pen along the page on the way to something new.

"Writing," Italo Calvino writes, "always means hiding something in such a way that it then is discovered."

———

I also suggest you find places to read your work aloud.

A chance to teach, lecture, lead a retreat, speak at a workshop—all these give writers a chance to write a piece we can read aloud to an audience so we can hone our skills and see if what we are writing is worth the time it takes for someone to read it. There is no better way to see how a longer work is coming along than to read a portion aloud to a crowd of unsuspecting folks.

When you read a work aloud, you can tell if the tone of voice holds up. You can spot the holes in a story more quickly. You can tell when the thing is slowing to a crawl and when it is moving too quickly.

You can tell whether or not people are laughing in the right spots or reaching for their tissues when you hoped they might. You can tell when the work drags and when the work sings.

If you read your work aloud and you cannot tell any of those things, you may want to take up watercolors.

———

I also encourage a writer to say yes to almost anything that gives her a chance to practice the craft.

A blog creates a space where she can see if she can work quickly and in short spaces, teaching her not to waste her words and her readers' time.

Letters, whether delivered by snails or by e-mail, give her

a chance to see if she can inform and entertain and challenge someone. I have long felt that if a writer cannot write a letter that will move someone, writing a book that moves a lot of someones may be too much to expect of her.

A column in a paper, large or small, takes a writer beyond herself, helping her learn to write for people other than herself.

———

"Are you still writing?"

"Yes."

Some days I hit off the tee, some days I play soft toss, some days I take batting practice, and some days the game is on. Some days I work in my home park, the little room at the back of our garden. Some days I am on the road. Some days I am reading, and some days I am copying quotes. Some days I am writing letters, and some days I am writing chapters.

There are no days when I am not working on the craft. There are no days when I am not a writer.

10

A Step in Time

On the Value of the Literary Stroll

A poet is a poet for such a very tiny bit of
his life; for the rest, he is a human being,
one of whose responsibilities is to know
and feel, as much as he can, all that is
moving around and within him.

—DYLAN THOMAS, *On the Air with
Dylan Thomas: the Broadcasts*

IT TAKES A VILLAGE TO MAKE A POET.

And some portion of my arrival at my present state must be credited to Ms. Flatt, the English teacher I had in high school. Ms. Flatt was the first person outside my family who told me I could write. No small thing.

And she is the one who told me about Dorothy Wordsworth.

———

Dorothy was William Wordsworth's sister.

The first story Ms. Flatt told me about Mr. Wordsworth and Mr. Coleridge was how they spent many of their days walking through the Lake District of northwestern England, dictating their poetry to Dorothy. I say Ms. Flatt told me the story. The class had a couple dozen other students, so it was not exactly a private lesson. But there is a possibility I am the only one in the class who has never recovered from her telling the story.

Mr. Wordsworth and Mr. Coleridge wrote much of their literary-landscape-changing poetry while walking through the landscape of Cumbria in the north and west of England. The vision of their poetical strolls stuck in my head for a long time. I could even see myself walking along with them, walking stick in my hand, a sturdy hat on my head, a good friend by my side, and my own Dorothy to scribble down my work as I dictated great poetry.

The closest I have ever been to the Lake District was when I was in my twenties. I was traveling with my family, and we were only a hundred or so miles away, but I could not convince the rest of the group that the journey across the Midlands might be worth the trip. I have been unhappy with myself ever since for not having been more persuasive. Though once I saw photographs of what hiking through the Lake District actually entailed, the city boy in me realized I was better suited to imagining the walk than walking the walk.

The group may have saved me from myself.

I do stroll around my neighborhood, though, with a walking stick that belonged to my grandfather and a hat on certain occasions. Alas, no Dorothy follows along scribbling down my sentences. Even the notion of such a thing makes me laugh at myself now, and rightly so.

Walking around helps me do several things. I have even been known to walk my way into moments of clarity.

———

A phenomenon known as writers' brain frequently visits our house.

A writer discovers the affliction is upon him when he forgets to put up the windows in the car overnight or goes out the door wearing mismatched shoes. Not being able to remember the supper plan or the day of the week provides a clue as well. An appointment goes unattended, a call goes unmade on the day arranged.

The condition is brought on by being so far down inside his work that the writer has lost sight of the world in which he works.

To the walking stick, I say to myself.

———

The stroll to my favorite coffee shop is twenty minutes long. In the forty-minute round trip, I will generally run into at least six neighbors, pass three or four construction crews, stop at two neighborhood announcement boards, wave at the people at our local mosque, look in the window of several small businesses I patronize, and stumble upon a couple of goings-on I never noticed before.

A stroll around the entire neighborhood, about an hour's walk, and everything goes up exponentially—a park, a half-dozen churches, a university, an elementary school. I have to watch out. The chances for overstimulation are high.

But I never have to walk far to realize that the writing I am working on, this most important writing ever done in the history of the universe, is suddenly not even the most important work going on in Sunnyside. The real lives of the crowd of people to whom I have been given and who have been given to me represent the real lives of the people for whom I write. To forget about them may well mean I miss the point altogether.

Staying hunkered down in my studio, writing as hard as I can, being immersed in my writing, is often necessary. Deadlines need to be met. Marks on the calendar are there for a good reason. Finishing the day's words or getting to a certain spot in the rewrite on a given day is part of the discipline of being a writer.

But recognizing my place in the world in which I live is another discipline that must be maintained.

Strolling through Sunnyside is not as romantic as walking the Lake District, but it can be valuable nonetheless.

—

Joe lived next door to us for a few years.

Our connection went a bit deeper than our neighborly conversations over a backyard fence. Joe worked in the printing business. He and I both knew about color separations and film and printing plates. We knew what it meant to hold up bits of film in the air and look at them through a loupe to see if what was about to be printed reflected the art the artist had hoped to make. We knew the smell of the acid on the plates and the smell of the ink on the press. Joe and I were printing and publishing dinosaurs together.

Joe had a concrete slab of a porch on the back of his house. He covered the porch and put a couple of waterproof sofas out there and a television on which he watched the Braves games in the summer and the NFL games in the fall and winter. I think of it now as the original outdoor man cave.

I used to wander over and watch Braves games with him.

Joe's manner of speaking was always very direct. One of our first conversations as neighbors took place when I noticed him standing at the fence, watching me put in the raised beds for a kitchen garden in our yard. It was the fourth garden I put in that summer, after the hydrangea garden, the rose garden, and the shade garden at the end of the house. I was busy overwhelming the gardener I live with by digging as hard and as fast as I could. I put my shovel down and went to say hello to Joe, certain he was about to compliment me on my hard work.

"You have to stop," Joe said. "You are killing the neighborhood." He went on to tell me the rest of the husbands in the neighborhood had begun receiving more weekend gardening requests from their wives than Joe and his friends wanted to handle.

"You have to stop it," he said. And then he burst into that great nicotine-cured laugh of his.

I arrived on Joe's porch one night after having been away for a while. "Where the heck you been?" he asked, offering a beer and a cigarette—two things I always said yes to in those days, both of which I miss all these years later.

Without hesitation I launched into an enthusiastic review

of the rich week I had just spent in a monastic setting—
reading only the saints or the Scriptures, eating only simple
food, saying prayers four times a day, having no telephones
or television, scribbling in a journal for hours a day, walking
the labyrinth twice a day, and engaging in a total of five
minutes or so of conversation each day whether I needed it
or not.

"Why the heck did you do that?" Joe asked.

——

Remembering Joe reminds me that the priorities, aspira-
tions, concerns, and joys of the world around me may be
different from mine.

Remembering Joe reminds me to stroll around or have a
conversation over the fence from time to time with someone
whose life is different from mine. It helps me remember that
what I think is most important is often not even barely sig-
nificant to others. My work may be the center of *a* universe,
but it is not the center of *the* universe.

I do not like this truth, but I believe it. And I believe all writers need to recognize it.

———

Writers often use metaphors to describe their work.

Partly we do so because our work seems mere and illusory and unlike anything that could be called useful or honest or tangible or real. We use metaphors to describe our work partly because we hope someday we may choose a metaphor that reveals to us the real dimensions of our work.

People say they do not understand how we "creative people do it." We creative people do not understand it either. We often do not even understand why we attempt it.

"You don't put things down on paper to produce masterpieces, but to gain some clarity," writes Etty Hillesum in *An Interrupted Life.* Her time on earth was only enough for the one book before she died in a concentration camp during the Holocaust. The book is now recognized as a masterpiece. People pay attention to a young woman who scribbles a postcard and throws it out of a cattle car on the way to what she knows is a certain death, a postcard that says, "We left the camp singing."

I spend most of my time, metaphorically speaking, as a kind of explorer, out wandering around in the philosophical dark, lost in the spiritual woods, searching for a deep something I often cannot even name, following trails leading to dead ends and darkness as often as not. You may have heard me crashing around down there in the woods and did not know who or what was making all the racket. You may have heard me from up there on the road where you travel along in the sunshine in the actual world.

From time to time it is important to come up out of the woods, one might say, and visit actual people. Sometimes an invitation is issued for me to come and speak. I almost always say yes and head off to the wilds of a Carolina or Alabama or Texas or some other foreign land. Sometimes I just take a stroll through Sunnyside.

I miss the company of the saints around me and want to be in their number for a while, or I think I found something out there in the dark that others might find interesting. Not much of a joiner by nature, more comfortable alone than in company, I never stay up on the wide road in the sunshine for very long. I spend a little time in the sun, make sure I am still heading roughly parallel with the saints, and then I head back to the woods, back to blank pages and unformed sentences, back to ink stains and rewrite problems, to the beret and the ball cap and the fedora.

The spiritual life is not so much about answers as it is about better questions. Writing can be the same.

After a road trip or a stroll, I head back to the board, hoping to find at least a better question if nothing else. I head back, looking forward to the days when I might go marching along with others, or in my case scrambling along, toward Zion.

I need to walk my neighborhood to remind me I am not alone.

A trip to Texas or a stroll through my neighborhood cannot compete with a walk in the Lake District with Coleridge and the siblings Wordsworth, but it can at least keep me honest, keep my work in perspective, and keep me from feeling altogether lost and alone.

Those are never bad steps for a writer to take.

11

To Air Is Human

On Sharing a Work in Progress

———

I could not imagine who I would have
been without them, nor can I imagine
it to this day because they are in so
many ways a part of me still.

—FREDERICK BUECHNER, *The Sacred Journey*

THERE COMES A MOMENT IN THE LIFE OF ALL BOOKS when writers want someone else to know about the things they have been scribbling all these hours and days and weeks.

It could be they are so excited as the work begins to unfold that they can hardly wait to share it.

It can also be they are afraid of the direction the work seems to be headed, afraid they are hopelessly lost, afraid they have made a promise to themselves they cannot keep, and they need assurance the book they are making will be worth reading.

From time to time writers need to think out loud, to show a little bit of what they have to see if it will hold water.

They are still wearing their berets, perhaps, and need a little encouragement.

Remembering which hat you have on when you share your work is important.

———

After lo these many years, I have learned to be careful about discussing what I am writing.

I have four books I talked to death before I ever wrote them. I know other writers who can say the same. One of those books exists only as a set of scribbled notes on four pages pinned to the wall in the room where I write. Another of the almost books is forty-five thousand words in length, an abandoned book that took up the better part of my writing life for almost ten months. It rests in a banker's box upstairs in the attic underneath my luggage.

At times I hear writers say they are afraid of talking about what they are working on for fear someone will steal the idea. The better reason to be afraid of talking too much is because the idea might disappear on you altogether. A writer can go into her room one day to write, and the thing will be gone, the words and the notion and the momentum having been spent in the air instead of on a page.

⟨ I do not understand exactly how it happens, but I can tell you from experience a writer can keep talking about a book until she no longer feels the need to write the book she keeps talking about. A writer begins to believe the story has already been told to everyone who matters.

If writers must talk about their current work, they are wise to do so sparingly and only to people who will be kind and generous. If they talk to the wrong person too soon, the talking can kill the work before much ink lands on paper. ⟩

"I sometimes wonder," writes Esther de Waal, "if in the kingdom of heaven there is a great room rather like a vast lost property office, filled with parcels of every shape and form, unclaimed blessings, that God has given us and we have failed to notice, to receive and make our own." I wonder how many books have been lost to us because some poor sentence maker had the wrong conversation with the wrong person at the wrong time.

A writer tries to tell someone what he is working on, and the encouragement he hopes for is not forthcoming. There are long, uncomfortable silences in which the writer becomes aware that what he may be making seems less than interesting.

A few such conversations and the writer is easily convinced this is not a book he can write and possibly a book no one needs to write at all.

———

Next time you are around your reading friends, ask who wants to read a book written by an unknown poet returning to someone else's roots in South Dakota by way of Hawaii and a Benedictine monastery in Minnesota to which she has become a reluctant oblate.

Ask who needs a book by an English professor who decides not to go back to work, choosing instead to buy an old house in a small village in Tuscany.

Ask folks if there is a market for a book by an unknown English major in a small Virginia town, a book about a pond, for crying out loud.

Do we need a memoir from an unknown and not particularly good novelist who is about to become a monk?

With the wrong conversation at the wrong time, we would not have the works of Kathleen Norris or Frances Mayes or Annie Dillard or Thomas Merton or hundreds of others whose work sustains and informs and shapes the lives of untold numbers of artists of all kinds.

Constructive criticism has its place, but inviting criticism too soon can stop a work before it has barely begun.

———

Write, don't talk.

Books are meant to be written and then discussed. The other way round can be deadly.

"Talk uses up ideas," writes Doris Grumbach, from whom I learned to keep my mouth shut about what I am scribbling. "Only if I bury them, like bulbs, in the rich soil of silence do they grow."

———

Too many suggestions from too many directions too early and a writer can be devastated and unable to write for days, certain the work is no good and never will be. Too much talk too soon and the writer gets lost, causing the work to slow to a crawl.

When you are writing the first draft, whether you are using a fountain pen or a laptop, whether you are writing six hundred words a day or more or less, the first trick remains how to get to the end. You have to be sure no one's criticism, no matter how well intentioned or even accurate, keeps you from doing so.

My father used to say with a twinkle in his eye, "Never lie to me unless you think I need it." When you are wearing your beret, and you have to show your fresh work to someone so you can be reassured that what you are writing reflects what you hoped to write, be sure that person loves you enough to lie to you in case a lie is called for. Early on, encouragement is everything.

There will be time enough later for the truth you need to be told. There will be time later for you to hear it and accept it in order to make the work right.

"Cast aside everything that might extinguish this small flame which is beginning to burn within you," say the wise words from *The Art of Prayer*, "and surround yourself with everything which can feed and fan it into a strong fire."

Good advice for those who would learn to pray. Not bad advice for those who would learn to write.

"Art is prayer," says Joseph Zinker. And both need time to grow in the direction of the thing to which they are being drawn.

"Amen and amen," say I.

After I have worked my way along to the second or third draft, I will give a copy to a few people, usually members of the jury, to see what they think. I have my Yankees cap on by this stage and have probably been wearing my butcher's apron for some time.

Some of the people I show the work to or read to from the work are people who make books, but most of them are not. I am looking for different feedback from each of them. When I show the work to people who do not make books, I hope I will learn what drew them in, what left them cold, what confused them, what made them scratch their heads. I need to know what made them laugh, what made them weep, what made them think. I do not expect them to know how to fix what needs to be fixed. Knowing what to do next is the writer's job, and I am the writer.

Somewhere there may be people who do not make books but can read or listen to someone's new work and are able to see holes in the story and offer suggestions as to how to make the work better. In all the decades I have been writing, I have never met a single one. Readers can tell you what they like and what they do not like, what moves them and what does not, what made them laugh or cry or think. If what you have made does not do any of those things to them, they cannot tell you how to fix it, no matter what they say or how much they love you.

When it is time to do the repair work, I show the work to a professional. I have come to believe that only people who are involved in this work—publishers, writers, agents, editors, professional word people—are able to provide the constructive criticism helpful enough to a writer to make the work better.

For the record I also believe that when your car makes funny noises, you should take it to a mechanic; when your teeth hurt, you should visit a dentist; and when your glasses need to be changed, you should go to an optometrist. Your pastor or your best friend or your neighbor might get lucky on any one of the three from time to time, but odds are that someone who does the work all the time will be better at it.

———

One of the secrets to sharing a work in progress is to know whom you are sharing it with and what you want to learn from them.

When you need encouragement, show it to people who love you. But do not ask them to do something they do not know how to do. Do not ask a friend to be your editor when she is only qualified to be your friend. Being a friend to a writer is no small thing, by the way.

But when you are in doubt about how others will react to what you have begun to write, it may be best to play the thing very close to your vest.

12

The Finished Line

On Knowing When a Work Is Done

This way of life brings us into touch
with the rhythm inherent in all things,
in the holding together of the contradiction
of growth and decline, of light and dark,
of dying and rising again.

—ESTHER DE WAAL, *Living with Contradiction*

"How is your new book coming?" someone will say. People think a writer knows.

"I hate the thing."

They always look at me with surprise.

"Don't worry," I say. "It means I am almost done."

I know I am finished with a book when I never want to see it again.

———

One of my hopes for those who would write is that they get far enough along to know the joy of the moment when they hate what they are writing, as odd as the notion sounds. The arrival at the moment when writers hate the book they are writing means they have wrestled their way through a first draft—and the next four or five or six. They have wrestled all the way to the end, working along at whatever rhythm and pace they have discovered works best for them. They have discovered the first draft is more of a beginning than an end, and they have made the choice to carry on despite whatever obstacles turned up along the way.

Their berets went back on the shelf at the right times. They held a little ceremony or took a few dance steps.

They got up the next day. And then they started to do the next part of the work. And then they finished it off.

———

Finishing means they shoved their gamers down tight on their heads for the necessary number of days and weeks and months.

It means they spent some of their days digesting the pages the way a reader might, two to three hundred words at a time, knowing that if the writer cannot keep the writer turning the pages, there is little chance of keeping a reader turning the pages.

They spent time reading it to themselves and listening for the voice and the feel and the rhythm of the writing. And moving a piece to another page and switching sections around. They fell into a hole between chapters and realized the hole must be filled before the book can go on. They discovered that some cherished bit does not belong in this book after all and must be cut away. They spread out the pages on the table or the floor and sorted them for the second time or the twenty-second time, knowing there was a crack somewhere and the thing would not be done until the crack was patched.

"He who would do good to another," writes William Blake, no stranger to writing worthy of being loved, "must do it in Minute Particulars."

We who would write must love the work in particular ways—each phrase, each sentence, each paragraph, each story. Until we cannot stand to be in a room with it anymore.

———

We hold the fair copy in our hands, all clean and shiny, looking for all the world like a book, a book the jury might accept, a book a crowd of unknown people might like to read.

We have loved the thing all the way to the end.

We picked up our colored pencils to have at it again, over and over, until deep down a voice muttered, "I hate this collection of sentences, and I never want to see them again. I wish I had kept my mouth shut and never told anyone I was going to write this. I am tired of listening to myself."

This is the moment when we just want this pile of ink and paper we have brought to life out of imagination and sweat and hope to go away and leave us alone. This is the moment when there is nothing in the world left to do but to let it go.

Congratulations. The work is finished. It is time to do a little dance. Have a long nap. Go for a swim. Go roll around in the September grass in the backyard.

Tomorrow it will be time to put on the fedora and find it a home.

And if you have worked at it long enough to hate the sight of it, I promise you will come to love it again some sweet day. That is when you will know you did a writer's work.

———

This book is now finished.

Sylvia Plath, in a letter to a friend, passed on the quiet news of the weekend: "We stayed at home to write, to consolidate our outstretched selves."

It is time for you and me to do the same.

When the question comes, "Are you still writing?" I hope your answer will always be, "Of course I am writing. I am a writer."

That answer means you and I will always be traveling along together, even if our writerly journeys look different. Know I am honored to be walking along this road with you, even if our paths never cross.

Tomorrow the sun will rise, God willing, and it will be time again for us to go to our tables. It will be time to pick up the pen or turn on the machine or take up the colored pencil.

Tomorrow we will look our juries in the eye and continue telling them the stories we started out to tell. We will craft sentences that are honest and true. We will finish the day's words and be artful enough to leave ourselves in a good place to do the next day's work as well.

There are stories that must be told and must be heard, stories waiting on you and me to do the telling.

Tomorrow we will write, write and not waste time. We will make dark marks on the page, the gift to which we have been given, the gift that has been given to us.

———

Tomorrow we will go dancing again.

Dancing on the head of a pen.

On Gratitude

Along the way in this book, I have quoted other people. Not being a footnote sort of writer, the best I can do is offer a list of the writers in the order in which they appear.

I am grateful for being able to travel along with them.

John Updike, *Odd Jobs*
Annie Dillard, *The Writing Life*
Henri Nouwen, *The Living Reminder*
Paul Simon, "I Know What I Know" from
    Graceland
John Wesley, *The Letters of John Wesley*
Doris Grumbach, *Fifty Days of Solitude; Life in a
    Day*
Peter France, *Hermits*
Anne Truitt, *Daybook*
Vincent van Gogh, letter 136, September 24, 1880
Eric Maisel, interview on *All Things Considered*

Ezra Pound, quoted in *The Cambridge Companion to Ezra Pound*

Ty Murray, interview on *Dancing with the Stars*

Rémy Rogeau, *All We Know of Heaven*

Philip Levine, quoted in *The Hand of the Poet*

Horatio Alger Jr., from *Five Hundred Dollars*

Carol Ochs, in conversation

Frederick Buechner, *The Sacred Journey; Now and Then*

W. Somerset Maugham, quoted in *The Hand of the Poet*

Linda Clare, in personal correspondence

James Taylor, liner notes from the *One Man Band* DVD

Abraham Maslow, *The Psychology of Science*

Gordon Lightfoot, liner notes from an album

William Wordsworth, preface to *Lyrical Ballads*

Clive Barnes, quoted in the *New York Times*

Dag Hammarskjöld, *Markings*

Italo Calvino, *If on a Winter's Night a Traveler*

Dylan Thomas, *On the Air with Dylan Thomas:
the Broadcasts*
Etty Hillesum, *An Interrupted Life*
Esther de Waal, *Living with Contradiction*
Anonymous, *The Art of Prayer*
Joseph Zinker, *Creative Process in Gestalt Therapy*
William Blake, *Selections from Jerusalem*
Sylvia Plath, quoted in *The Hand of the Poet*

——

There are books I count on to help me make the books I
make. It is a list too long to be the proverbial deserted-island
list, but if I end up on an island, I likely will not have had a
chance to arrange transport for a lot of things I love.

The first list is my favorite books by the writers I mentioned and quoted throughout this book. The list includes
titles not named in the text.

The second list contains books full of bits and pieces

from all kinds of writers and books that help me discover writers—breviaries, devotional books, collections of quotes, books that feed the life of a writer. All of them open up different voices for me. I keep these books close at hand, in a stack beside my writing board, and pay attention to the writers I stumble upon in their pages.

Another group is a list of reference works I turn to all the time. One is the *Oxford English Dictionary,* all twenty-one volumes of which actually reside in our dining room, a generous gift from the woman to whom I am married. Leaving those volumes behind is a dismaying prospect to be sure, but one can count on only so many books for a deserted island.

———

Saint Benedict of Nursia
　　The Rule of Saint Benedict
Frederick Buechner
　　The Sacred Journey; Now and Then; Godric; Brendan;
　　The Son of Laughter; Listening to Your Life

Esther de Waal
Living with Contradiction

Annie Dillard
The Writing Life; An American Childhood;
Teaching a Stone to Talk

Louis Evely
That Man Is You

Shelby Foote
The Civil War, 3 volumes

John Gardner
On Becoming a Novelist

Graham Greene
The Power and the Glory;
The End of the Affair;
The Ministry of Fear; The Heart of the Matter

Doris Grumbach
Fifty Days of Solitude; Life in a Day;
The Presence of Absence

Etty Hillesum
An Interrupted Life

John Le Carré
The Quest for Karla (omnibus edition);
The Secret Pilgrim; The Spy Who Came in from the Cold;
A Perfect Spy
Thomas Merton
Thoughts in Solitude;
The Journals of Thomas Merton, 7 volumes
Patrick O'Brian
The Aubrey/Maturin Series, 21 volumes
Rainer Maria Rilke
Letters to a Young Poet; The Book of Hours
William Styron
Darkness Visible

———

Susan Bell
The Artful Edit
Bob Benson Sr. and Michael W. Benson
Disciplines for the Inner Life

Anne Fadiman
Ex Libris
Clifton Fadiman
The Lifetime Reading Plan
Rueben P. Job and Norman Shawchuck
A Guide to Prayer for Ministers and Other Servants;
A Guide to Prayer for All Who Seek God
Eric Partridge
Origins: A Short Etymological Dictionary of Modern
English
Laurence J. Peter
Peter's Quotations
Rodney Phillips, editor
The Hand of the Poet
Francine Prose
Reading Like a Writer
William Strunk Jr. and E. B. White
The Elements of Style

*The Book of Common Prayer of the Episcopal Church
    of America*
The Chicago Manual of Style
The Complete Parallel Bible
The Doubleday Roget's Thesaurus in Dictionary Form
The New English Bible

A Last Note

As solitary as the writing life can be at times, whether the solitude is self-imposed or a function of the fact the writer is often barely civil while working—I have experience with both states—a writer never works alone.

A writer has champions—such as Steve and Laura and Carol and a long list of others at WaterBrook, folks who keep grinning in his direction and give him a chance to make books.

He has friends—like Jan and Jim, who live in a house they are willing to share with him from time to time so he can finish a particular work, a house on Virtue Road, no less.

He has a wordsmith who is willing to spend a portion of her days each year helping him make his sentences and stories as good as they can be—Ms. Lil of Dorcester Lane to be exact.

He has someone who loves him and always cheers for him to be more Robert rather than less—Ms. Jones of Merigold.

And he is never poet enough to say to any of them how grateful he is.

About the Author

ROBERT BENSON lives and writes in Nashville, Tennessee. He travels from there to speak at conferences and retreats and other sorts of things around the country and would be more than happy to talk to you about coming to be with you and your crowd of friends.

He is happy for people to write to him at 1001 Halcyon Avenue, Nashville, TN 37204. He will even write back. And you are more than welcome to visit with him at robertbensonwriter.com and on Facebook at http://tinyurl.com/RBWriterFacebook.

Also Available from Robert Benson

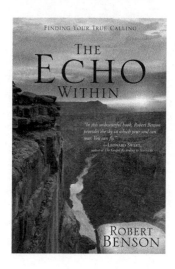

Delivered with wisdom and heart, a thoughtful, honest, often humorous, illuminating, and profoundly affecting look at finding and living one's vocation and calling.

Using personal experiences and insights, Robert Benson explores what threatens to keep Christians apart and how healing within the community can bind them together.

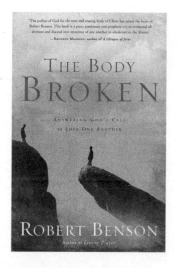

To learn more about these books and more, visit
www.WaterBrookMultnomah.com.

Discover what the struggle of creating a backyard garden can teach you about growing relationships with family, friends, and neighbors.

A Caribbean island and its people awaken a sense of place and home, prompting ideas about beauty, community, and the spiritual life.

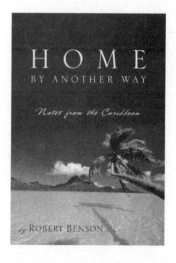

To learn more about these books and more, visit
www.WaterBrookMultnomah.com.